LINCOLN LOGS ™

Building Manual
Graphic Instructions for 37 World-Famous Designs

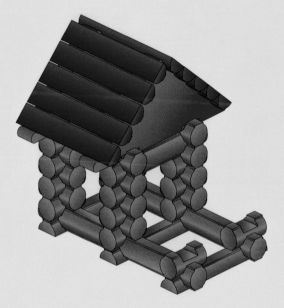

By Dylan Dawson • Illustrations by Robert Steimle

STERLING

New York / London
www.sterlingpublishing.com

STERLING and the distinctive Sterling logo are registered trademarks of Sterling Publishing Co., Inc.

Library of Congress Cataloging-in-Publication Data

Dawson, Dylan.
Lincoln Logs blueprint building manual : graphic instructions
for 37 world-famous designs / Dylan Dawson.p. cm.
ISBN-13: 978-1-4027-5077-9
ISBN-10: 1-4027-5077-3
1. Log cabins—Models. 2. Wooden toys. 3. Lincoln Logs (Trademark) I. Title.
TH4840.D39 2007
688.7'25—dc22   2007006755

2   4   6   8   10   9   7   5   3   1

Published in 2007 by Sterling Publishing Co., Inc.
387 Park Avenue South, New York, NY 10016

Distributed in Canada by Sterling Publishing
c/o Canadian Manda Group, 165 Dufferin Street,
Toronto, Ontario, Canada M6K 3H6
Distributed in the United Kingdom by GMC Distribution Services,
Castle Place, 166 High Street, Lewes, East Sussex, England BN7 1XU
Distributed in Australia by Capricorn Link (Australia) Pty. Ltd.
P.O. Box 704, Windsor, NSW 2756, Australia

Sterling ISBN-13: 978-1-4027-5077-9
ISBN-10: 1-4027-5077-3

Design by Pamela Darcy of Neo9 Design Inc.

For information about custom editions, special sales, premium and
corporate purchases, please contact Sterling Special Sales
Department at 800-805-5489 or specialsales@sterlingpub.com.

CONTENTS

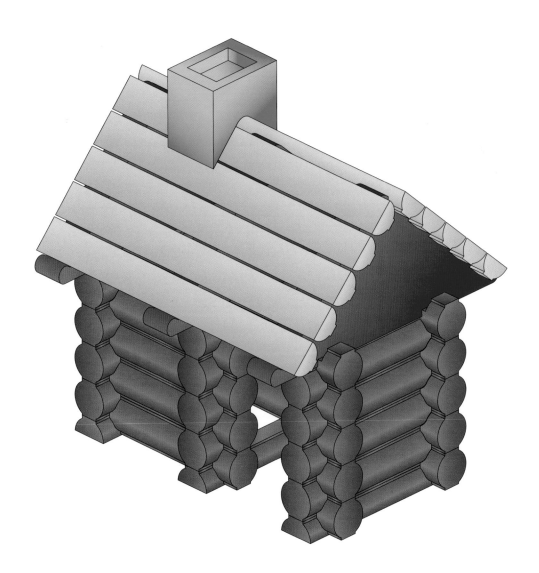

INTRODUCTION

LINCOLN LOGS™ building sets are a toymaker's dream. Invented by John Lloyd Wright, son of architect Frank Lloyd Wright, these sturdy, interlocking logs are over 90 years old. They challenge children's powers of concentration and eye-hand coordination.

This book is full of colorful illustrations that take you step by step through 37 stimulating designs like an old time Fort and Fire Station. The projects are ordered from easier to more challenging so you can choose which ones you want to try first. We have placed numbers within the steps to help guide you as you go. Each corresponding number connects to the other. You can start with a neat Arbor and work up to an impressive Bell Tower! You may need more than one set to complete some of these, so make sure you've got some extra pieces before you begin.

We've included a CD-Rom that shows how to assemble each project, so you'll be able to follow along on your computer as you put together these amazing designs. This CD works on both Macintosh and PC computers. To use, just insert into your computer, browse to your CD drive and view the contents. Double-click on the file named "START" and you are all set!

Arbor

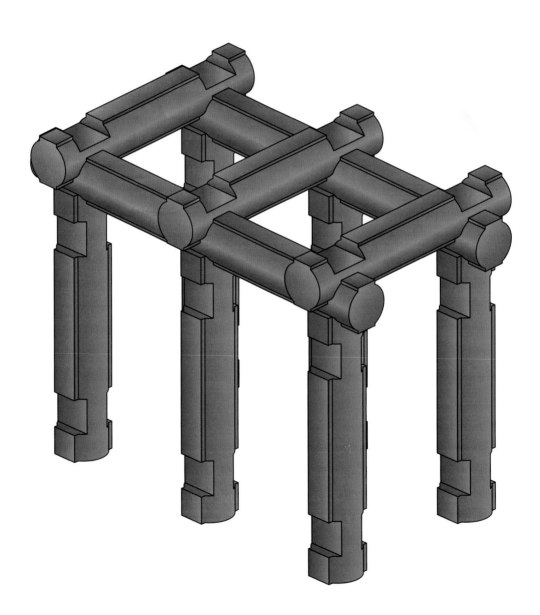

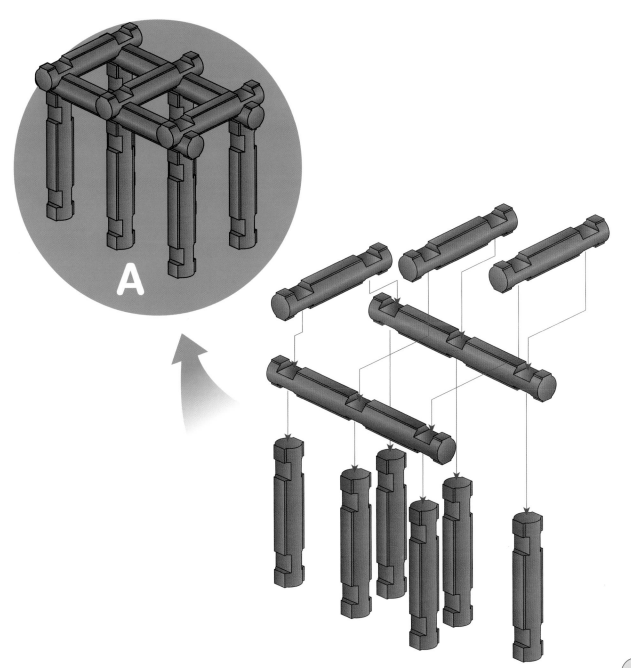

Washboard

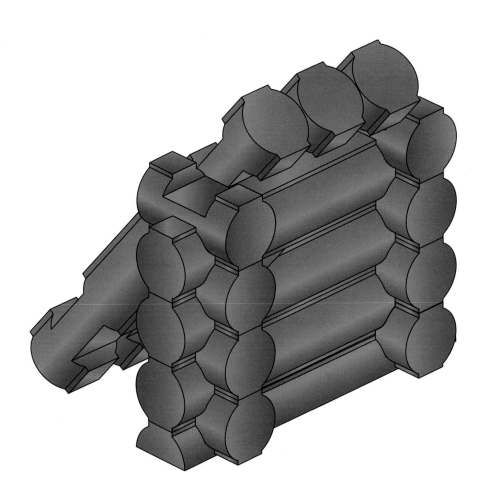

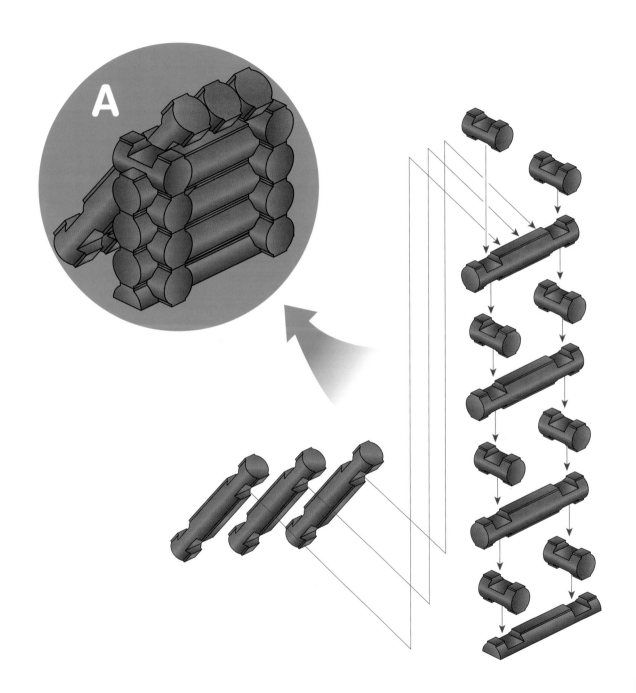

Root Cellar

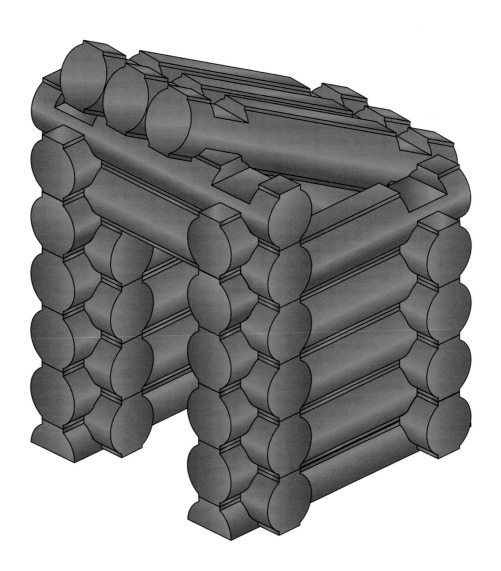

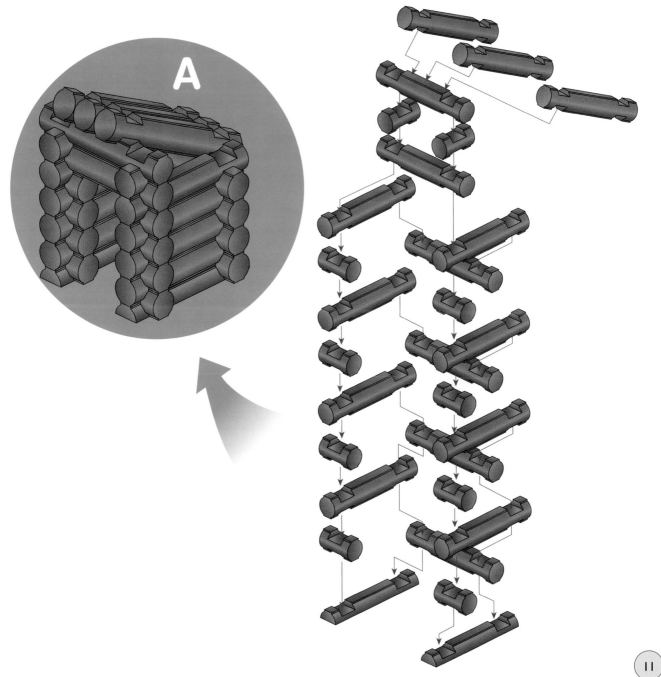

Chicken Coop

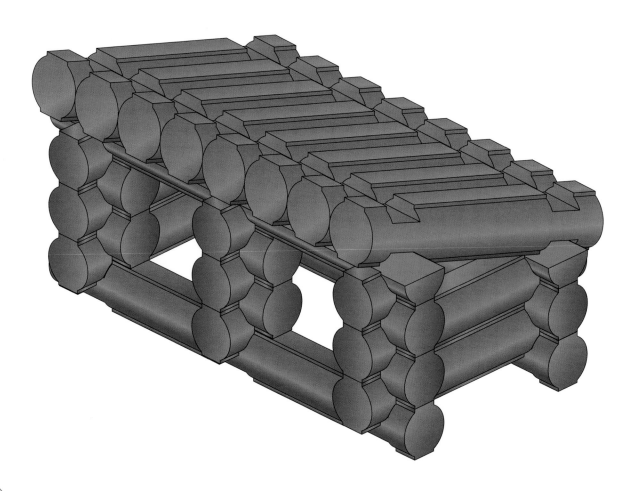

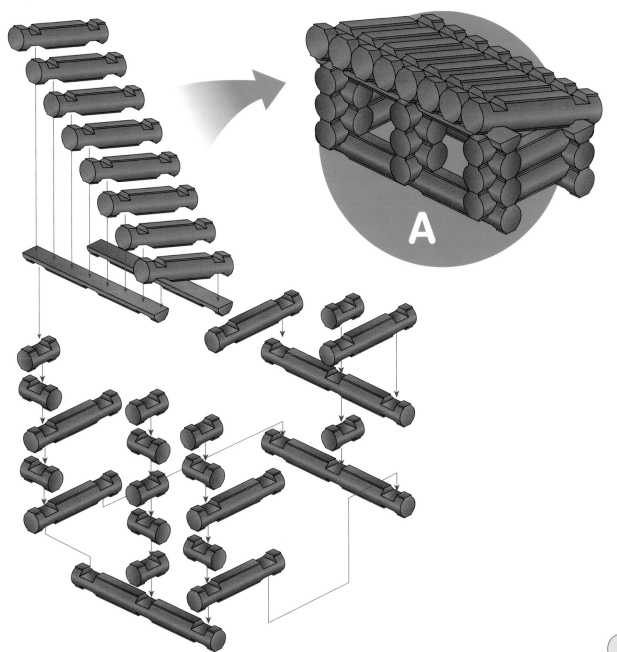

The Opry

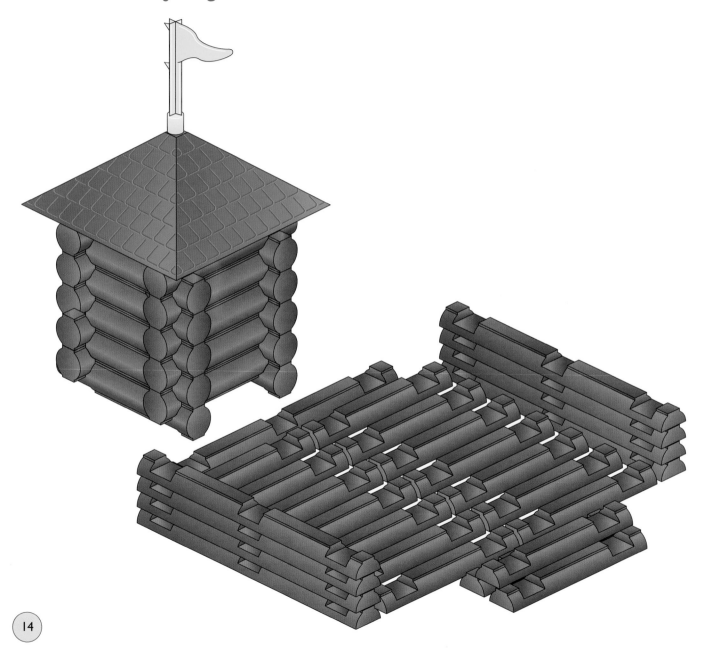

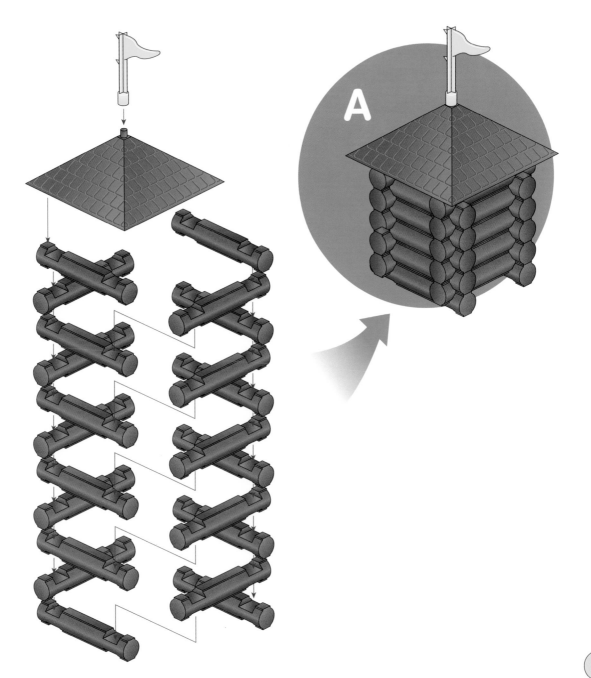

Corn Crib

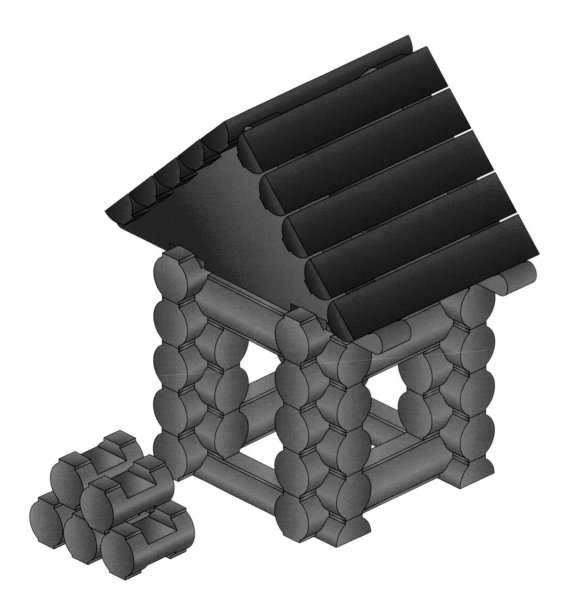

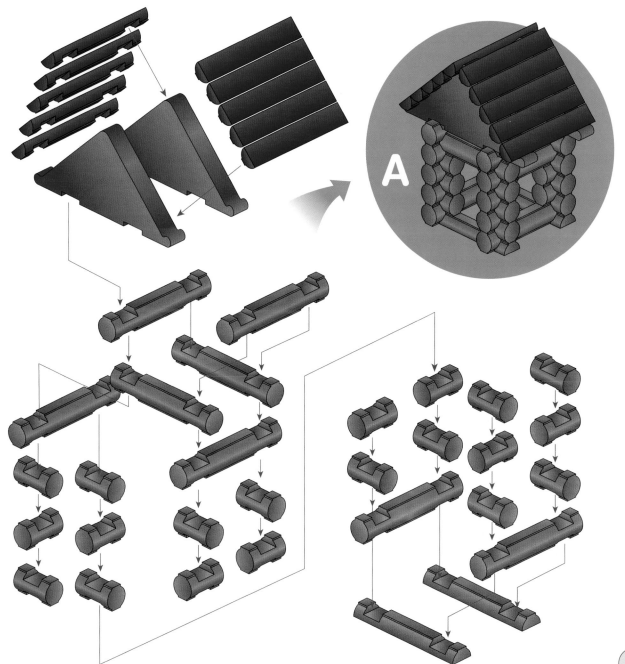

Horse Corral

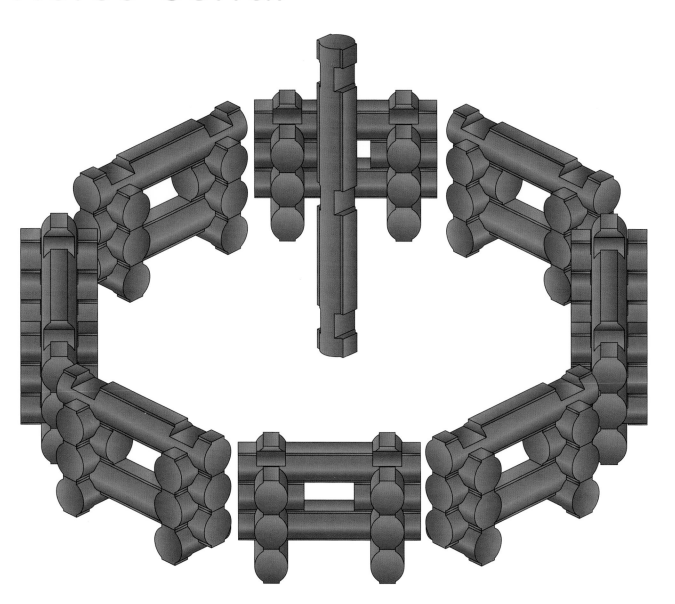

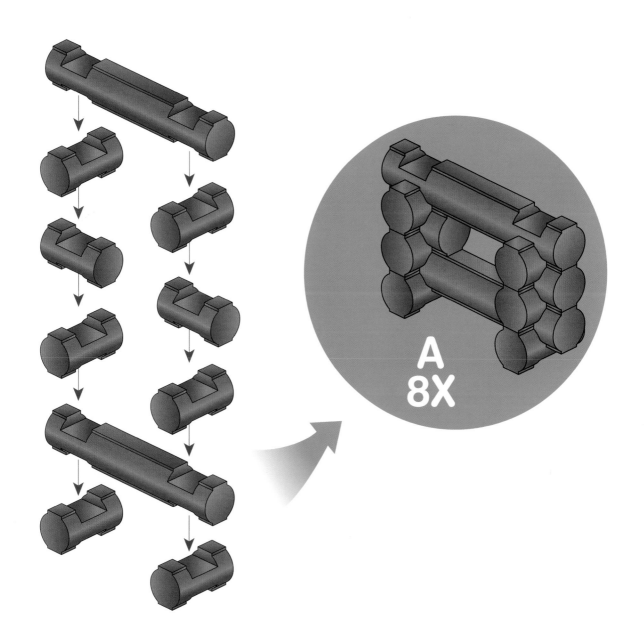

A
8X

Horse Fences

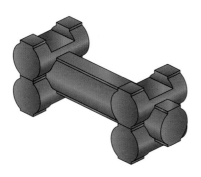

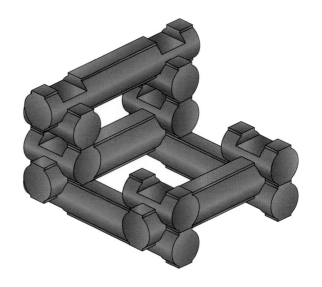

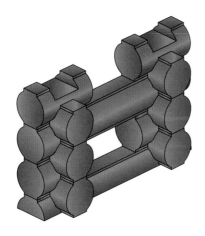

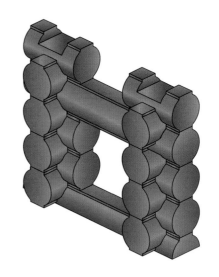

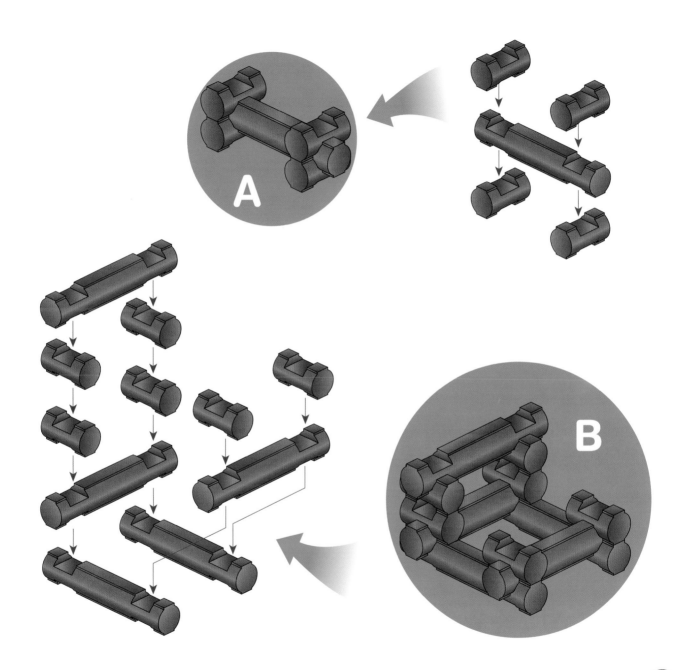

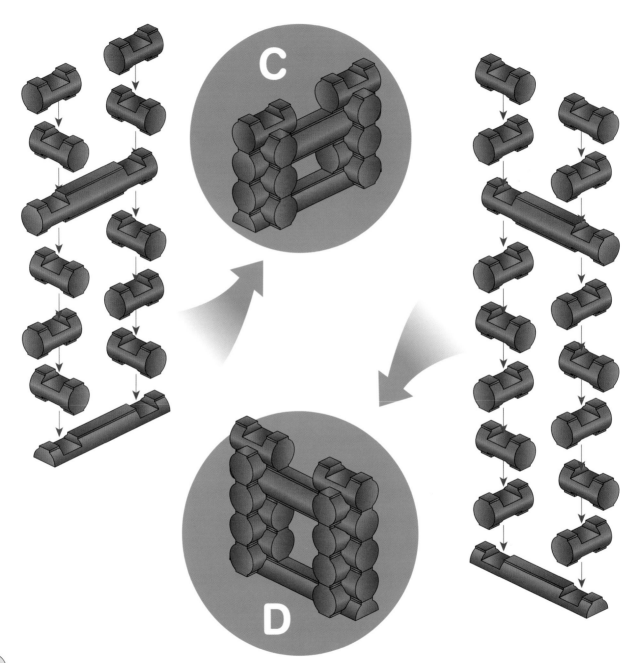

Ramp

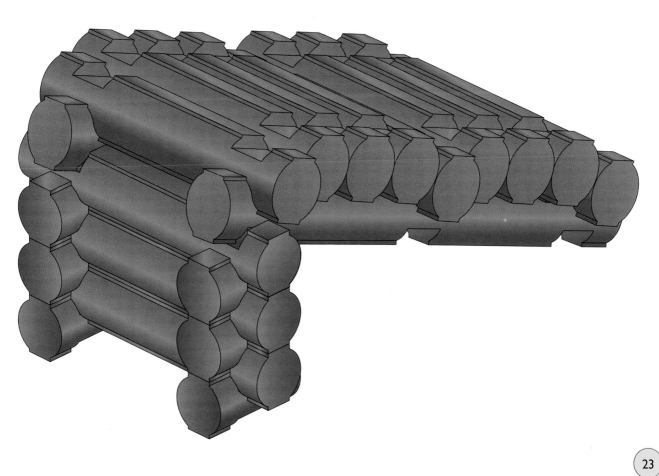

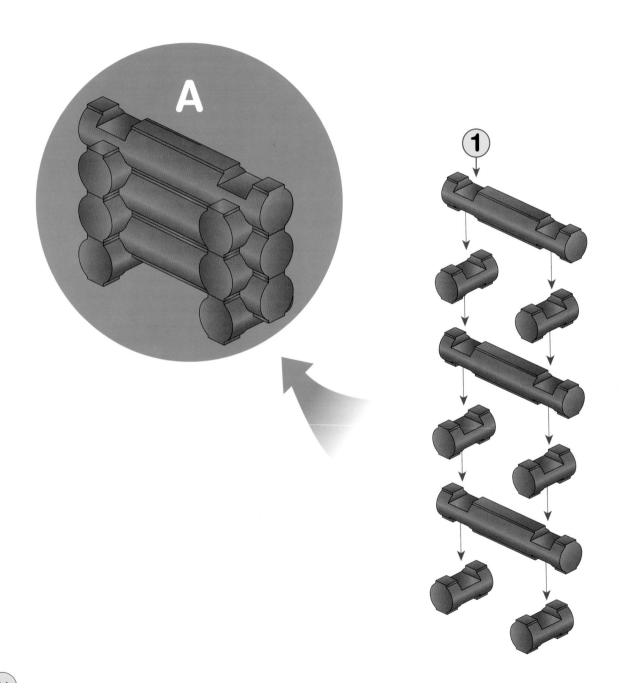

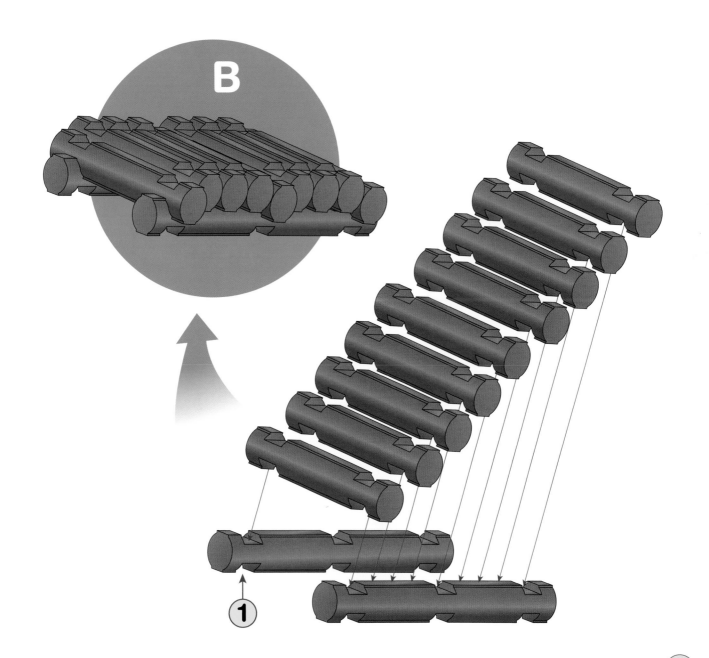

B

1

House

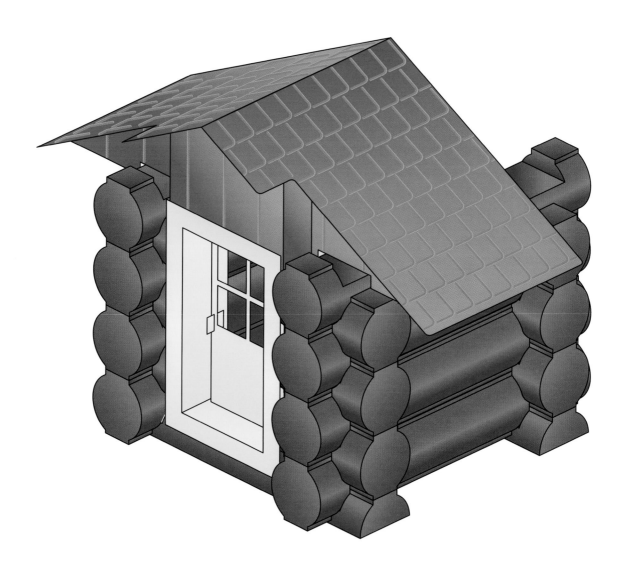

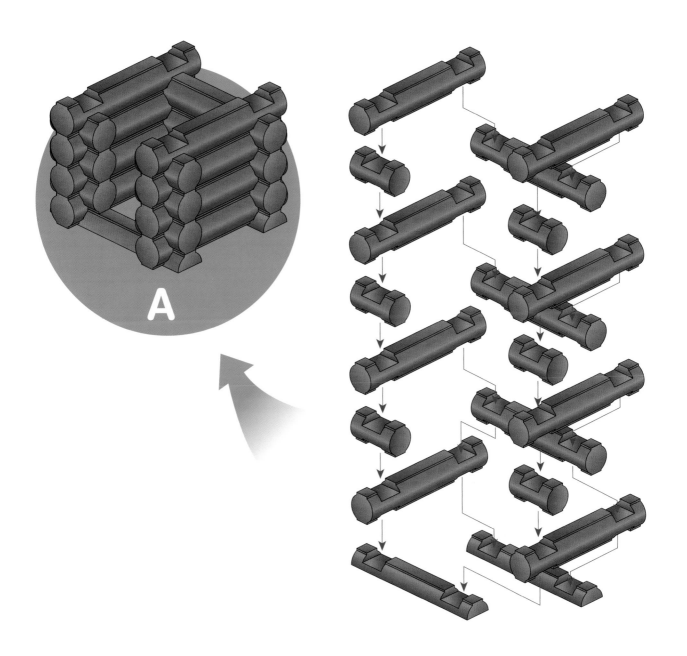

A

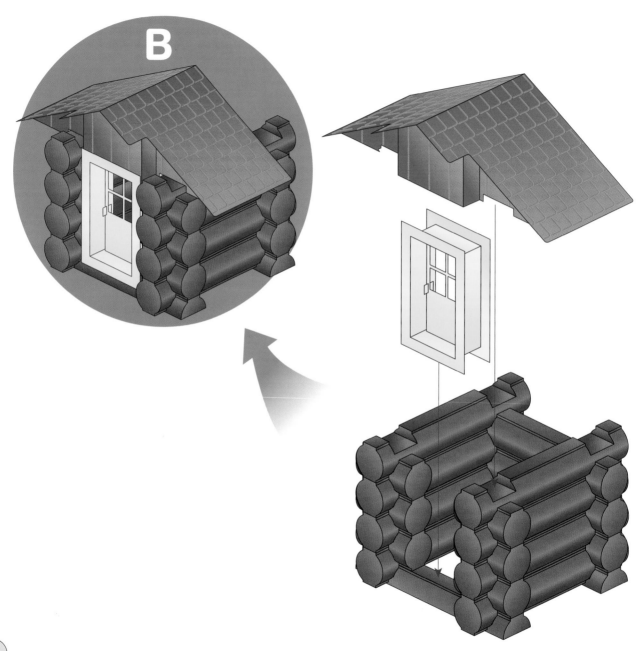

Well

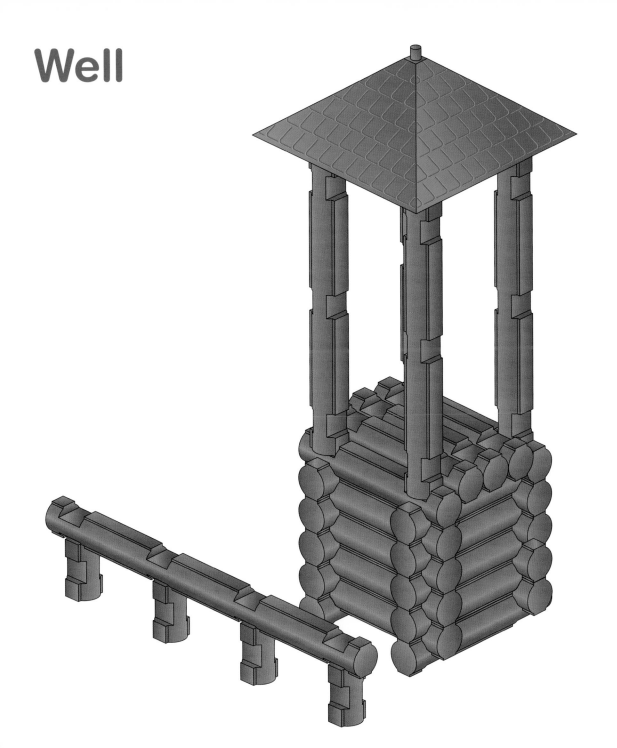

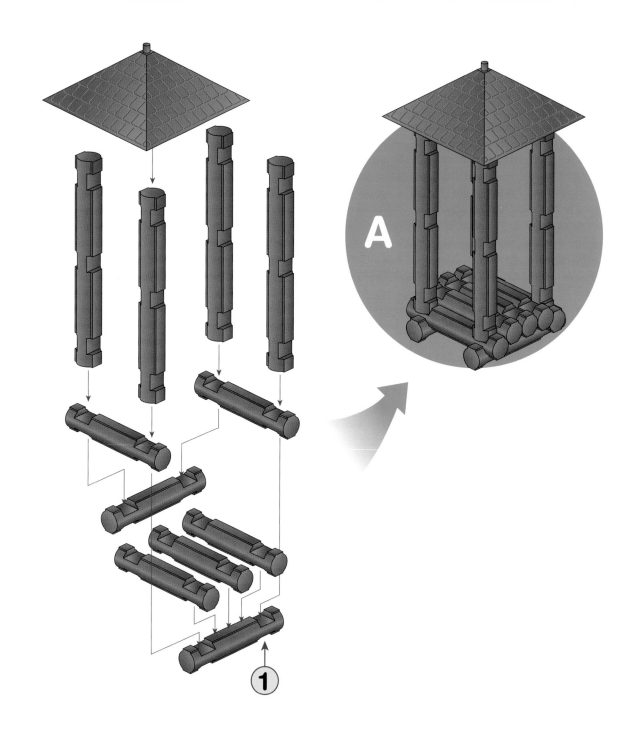

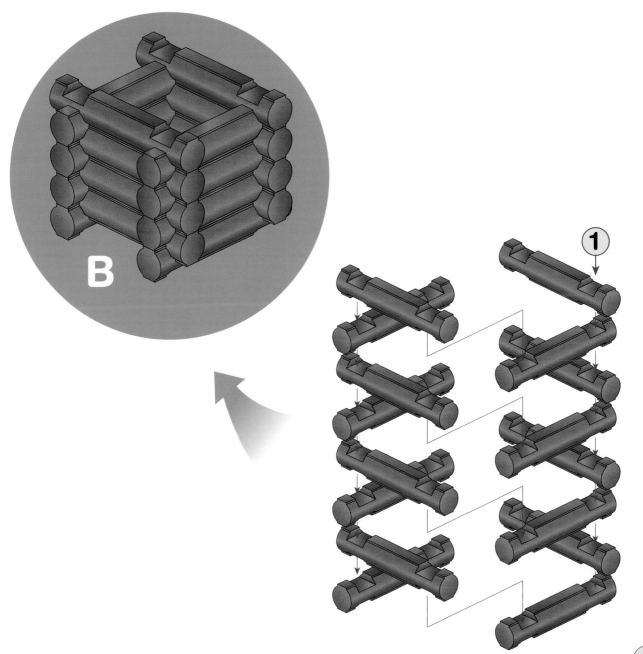

Shed

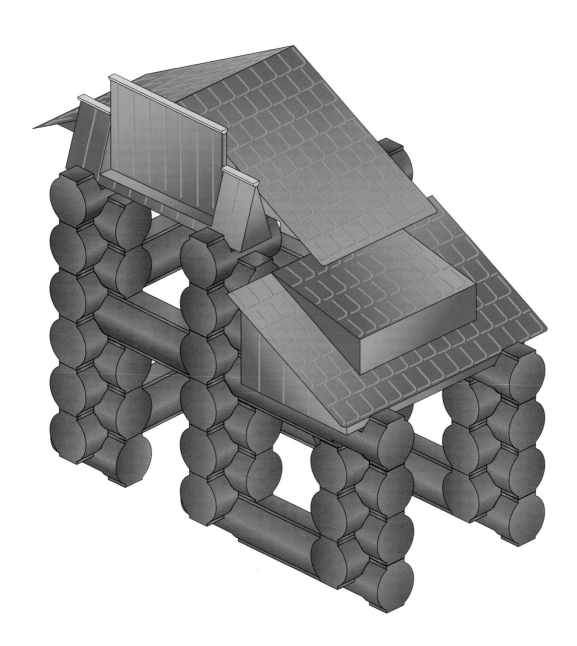

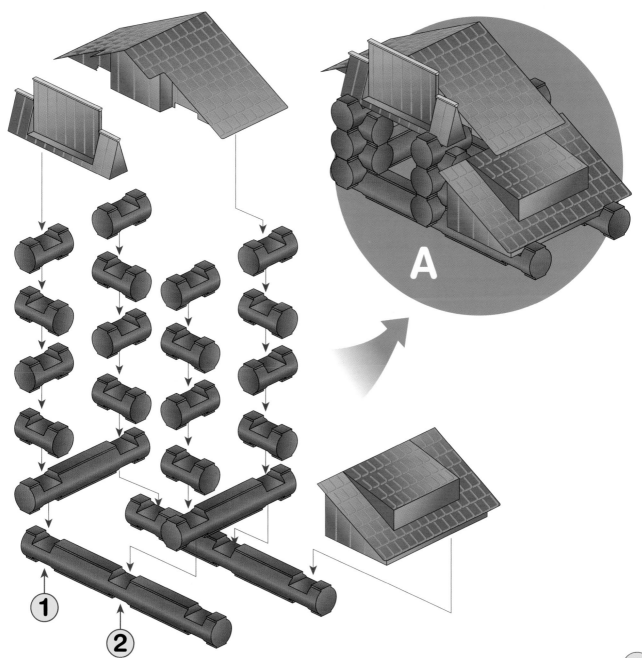

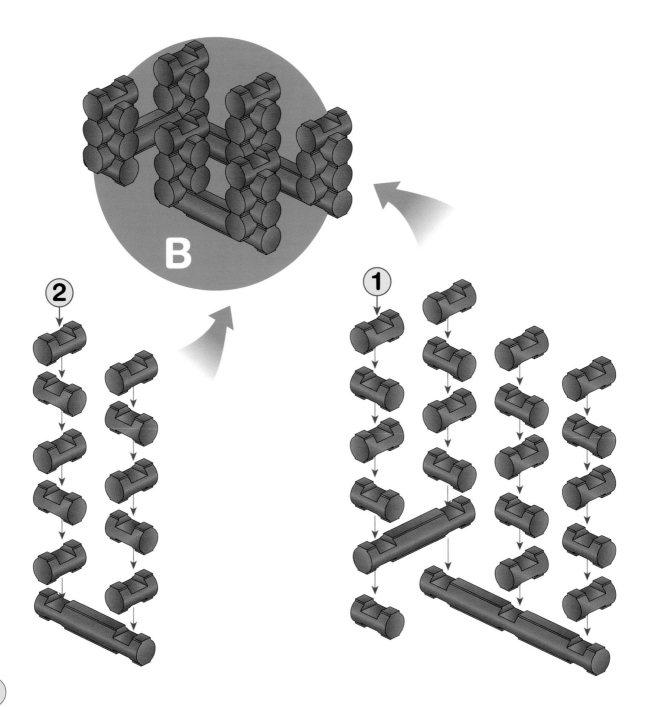

Stage

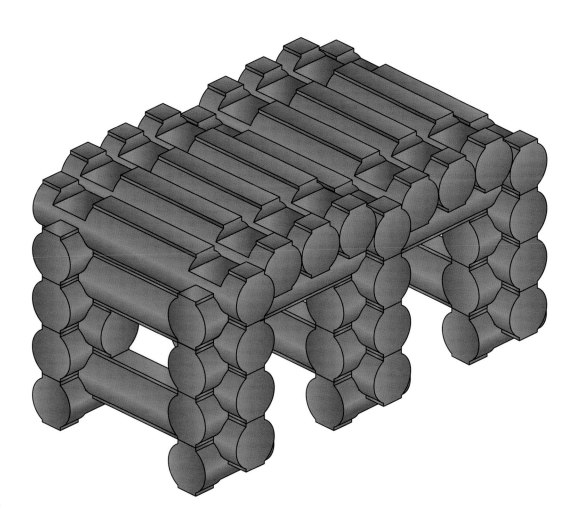

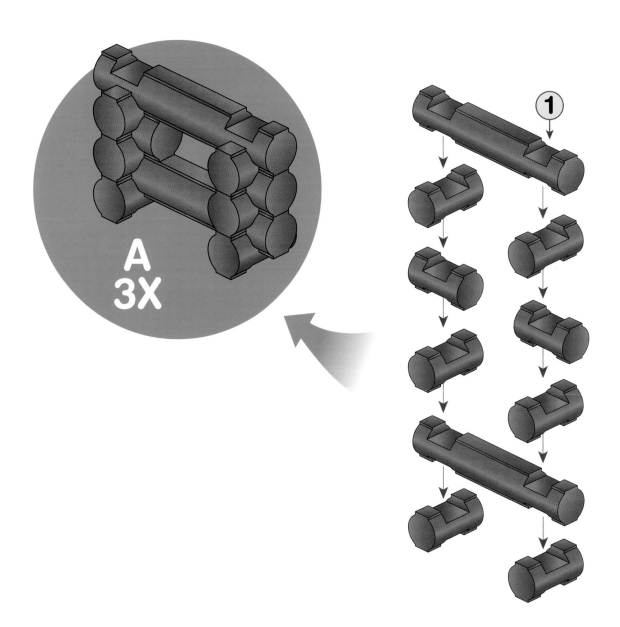

A
3X

1

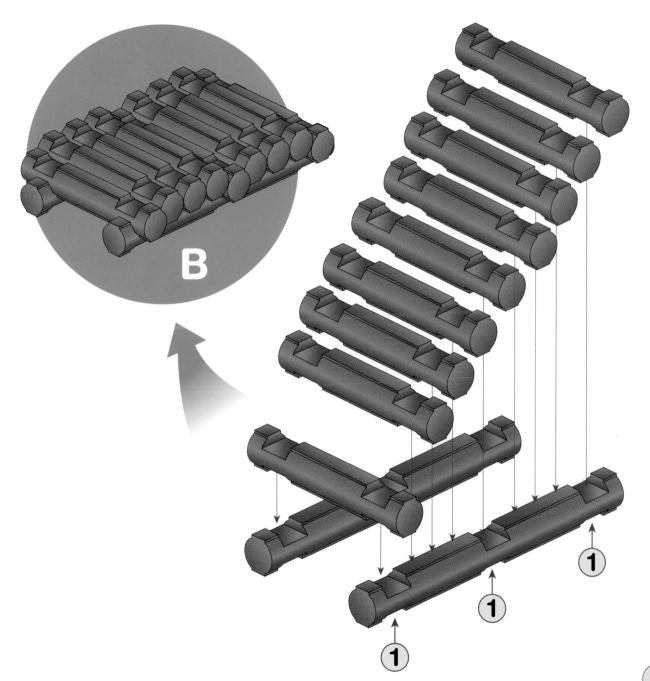

Dock

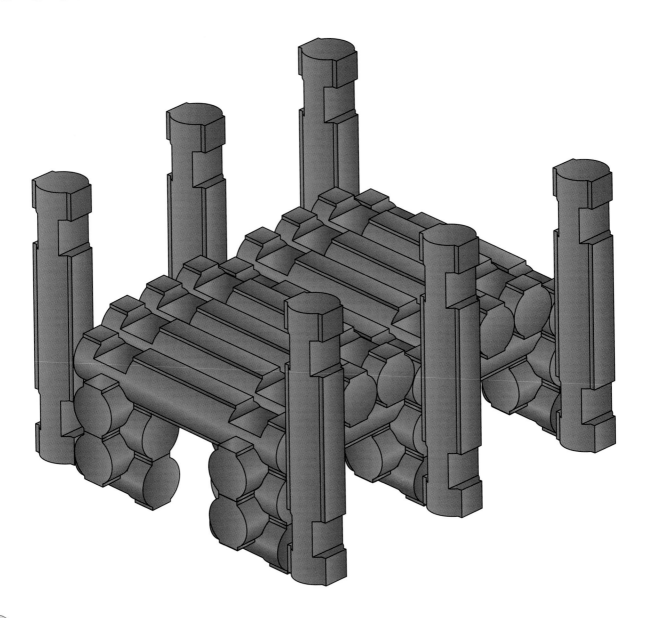

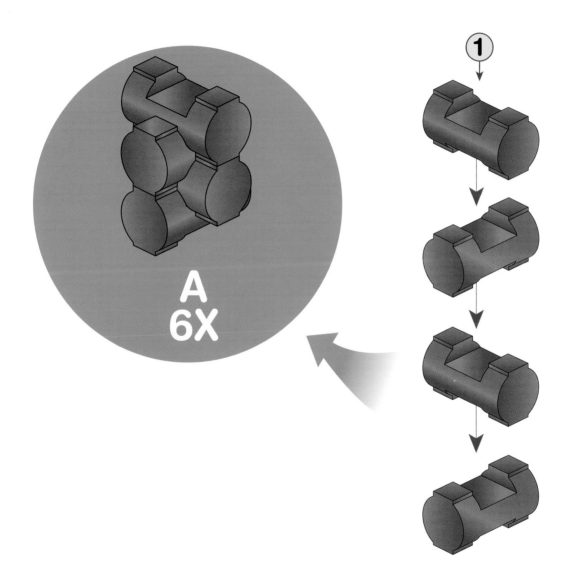

A
6X

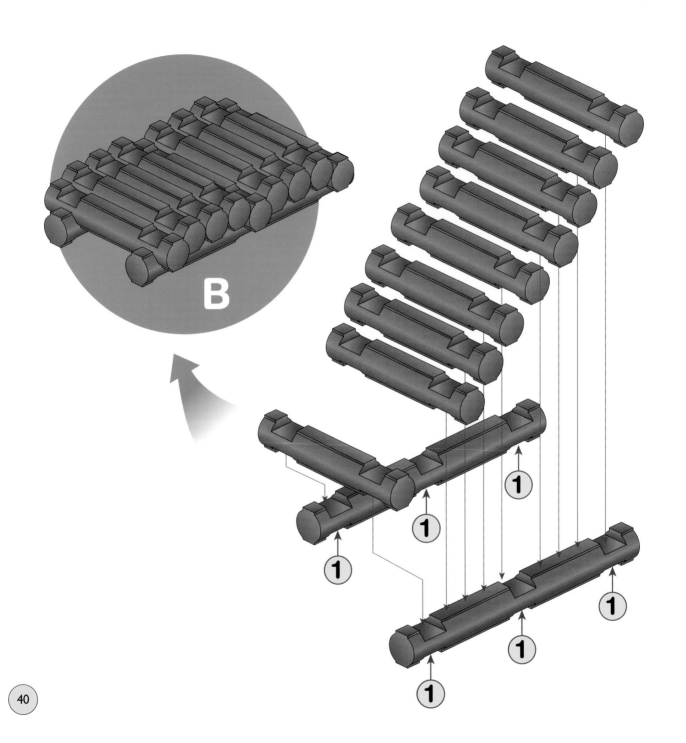

Fort

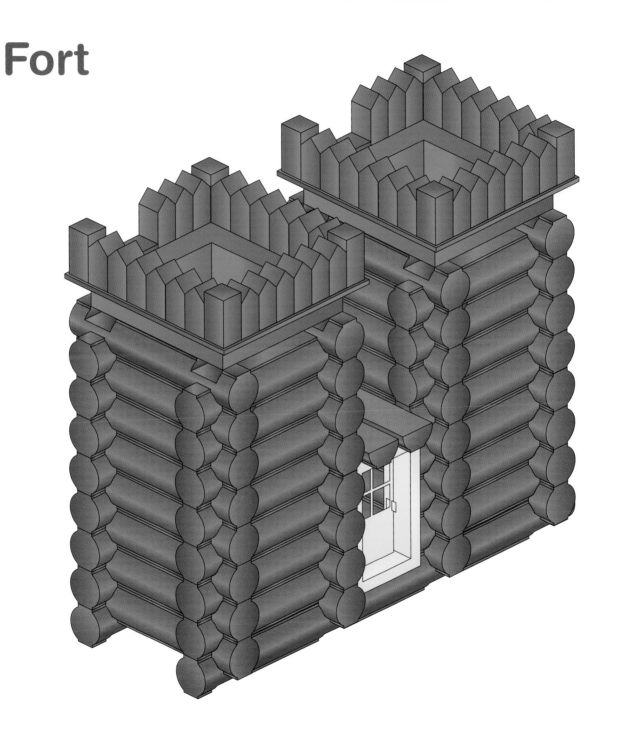

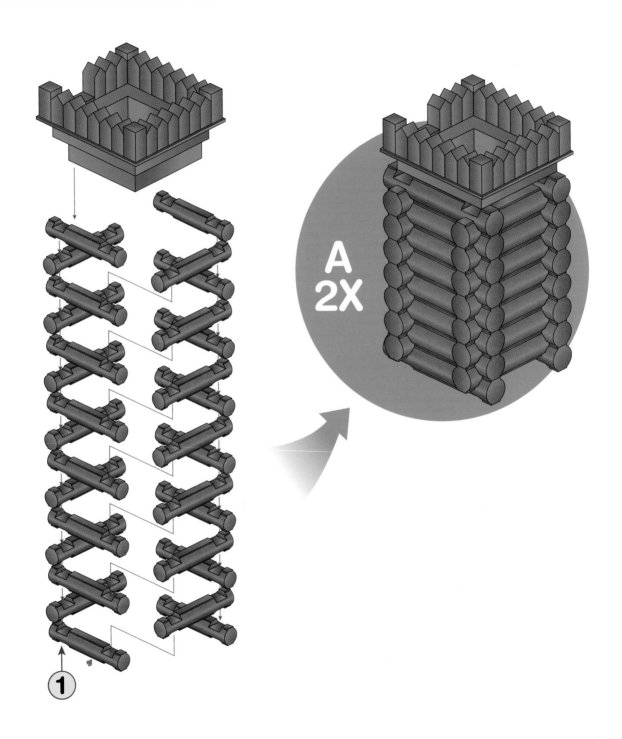

A
2X

1

42

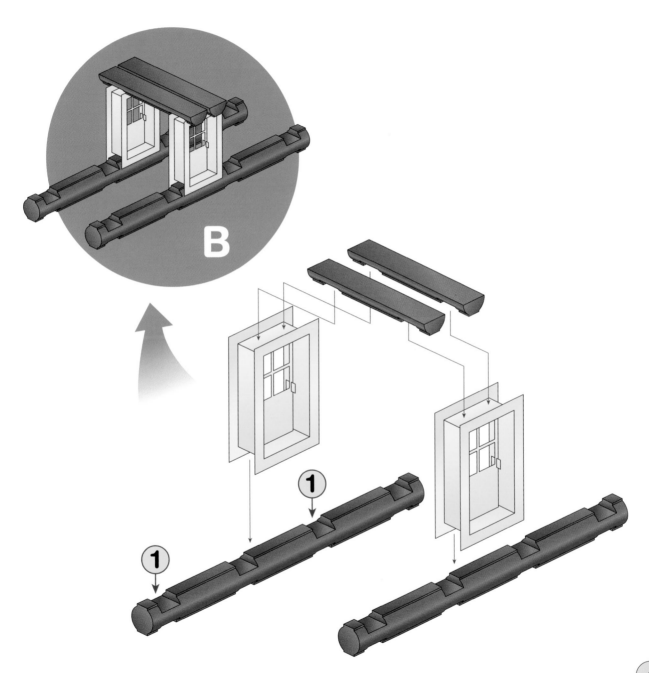

B

1

1

43

Gazebo

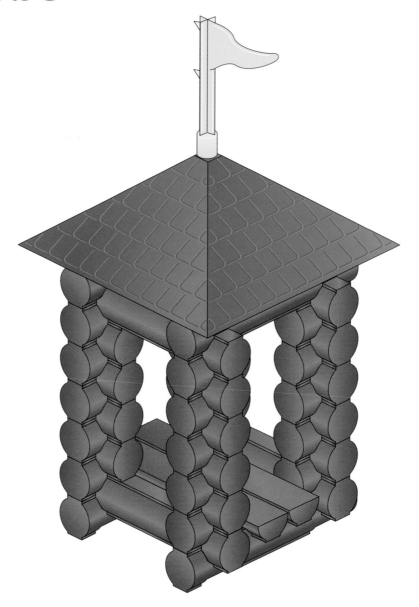

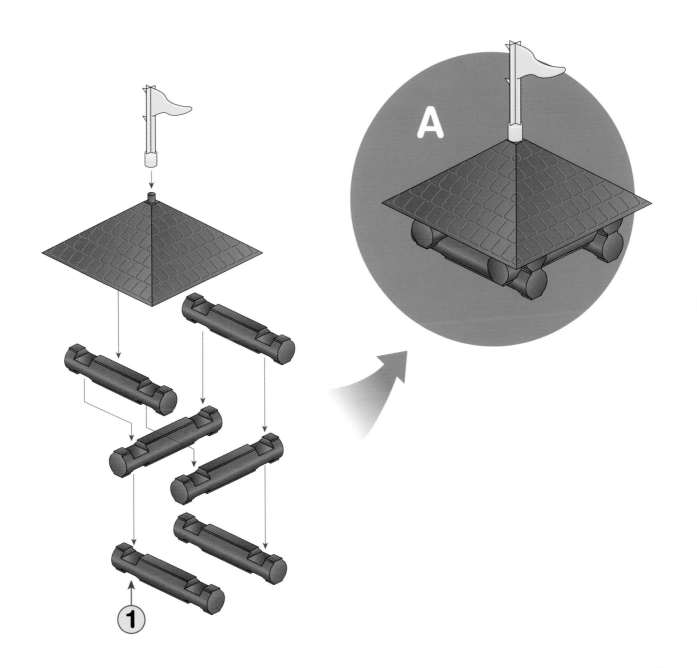

A

1

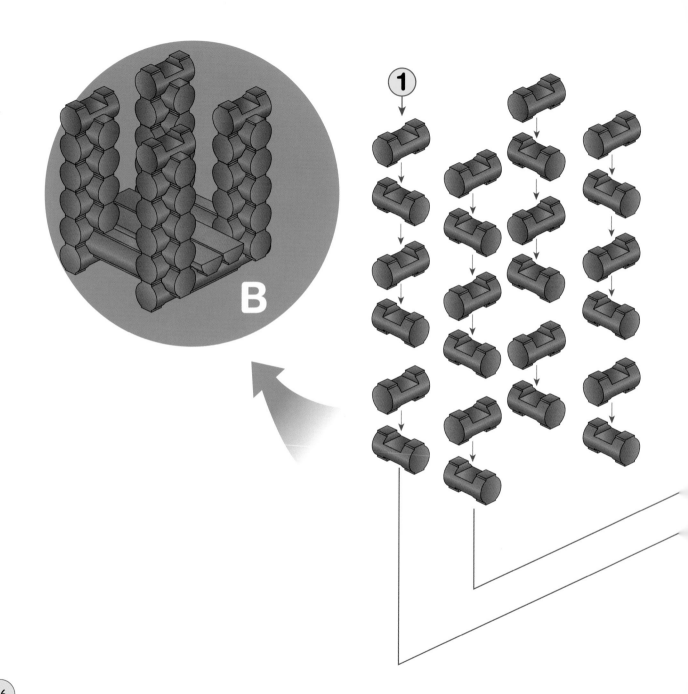

B

1

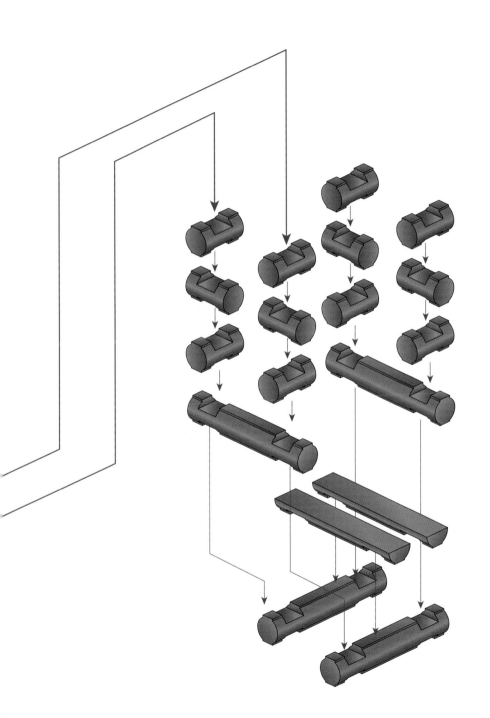

Cabin

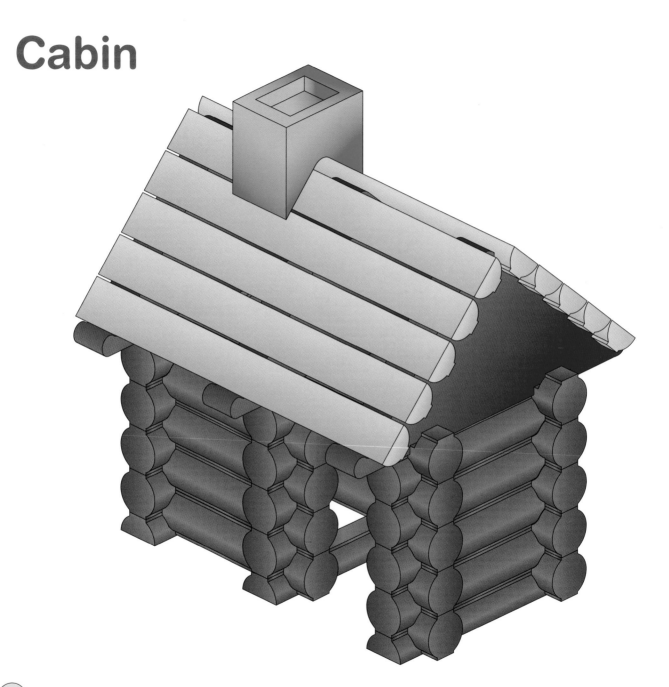

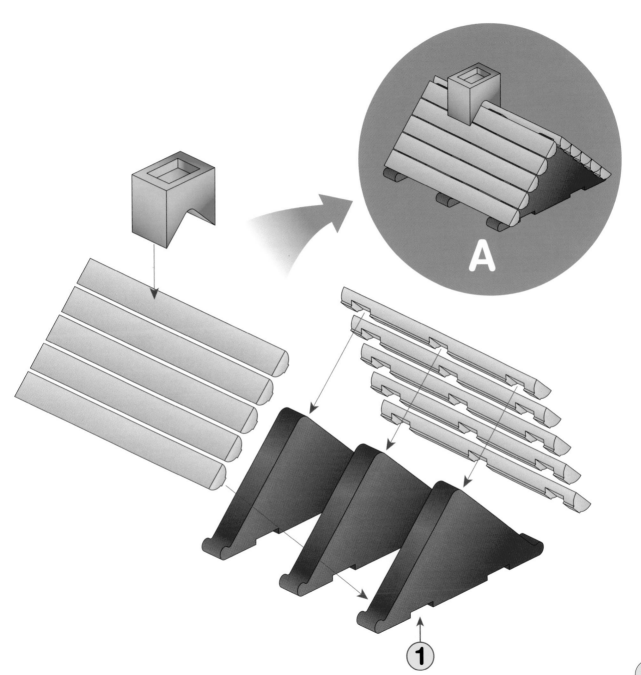

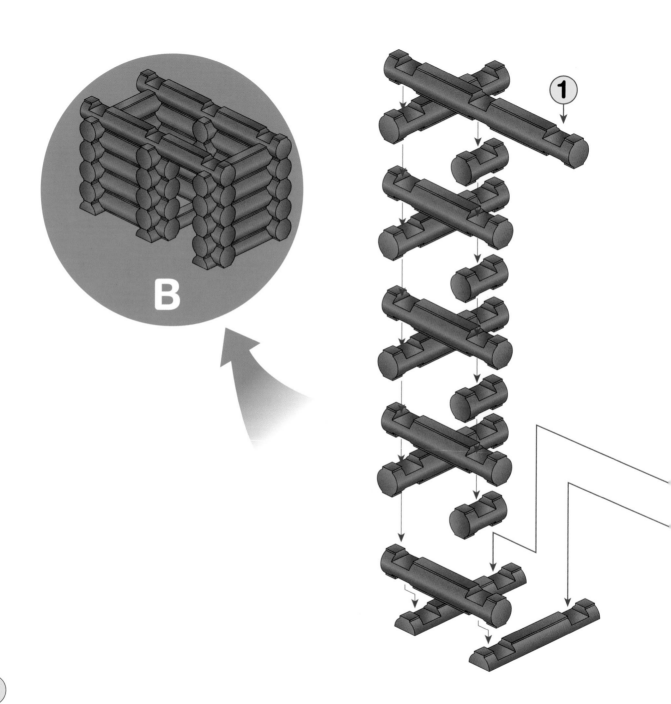

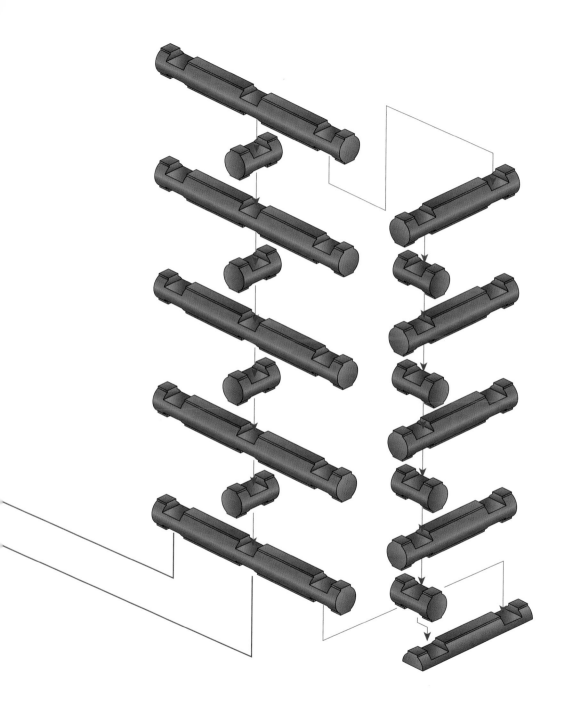

Bridge

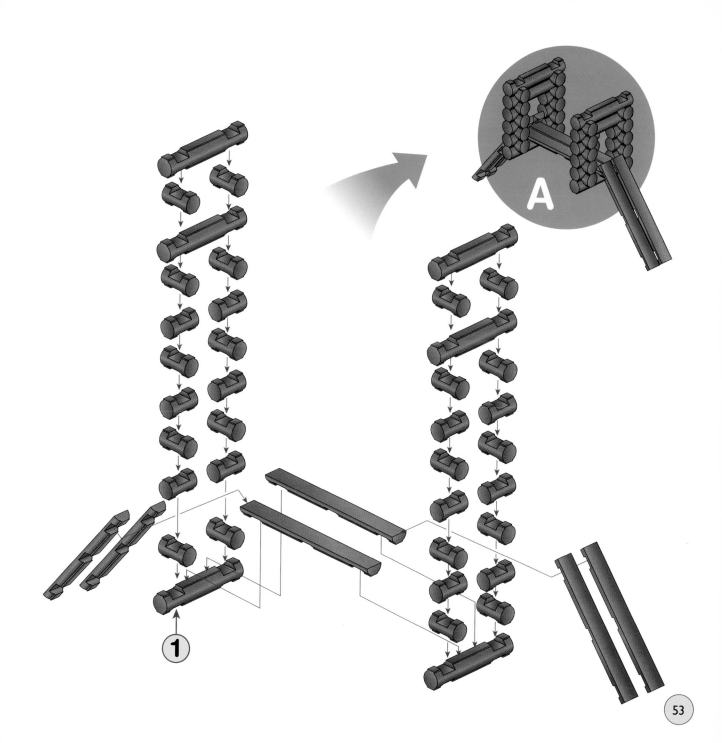

A

1

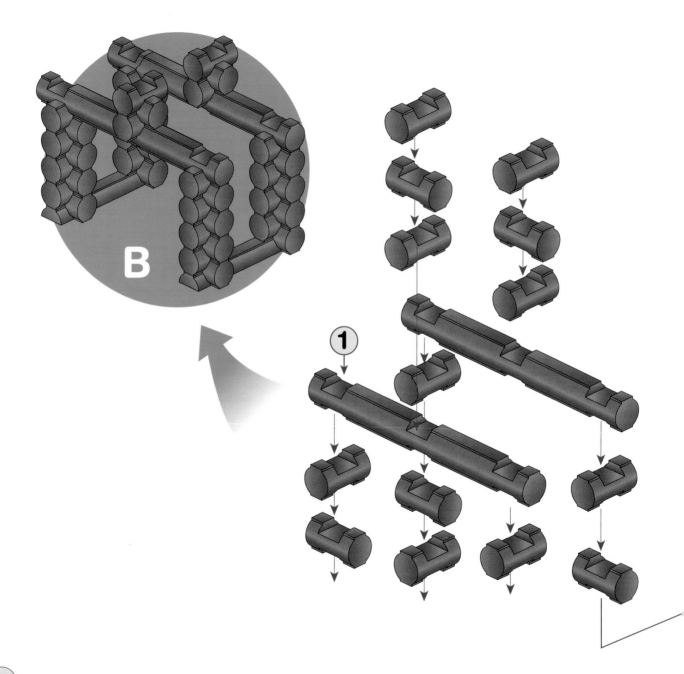

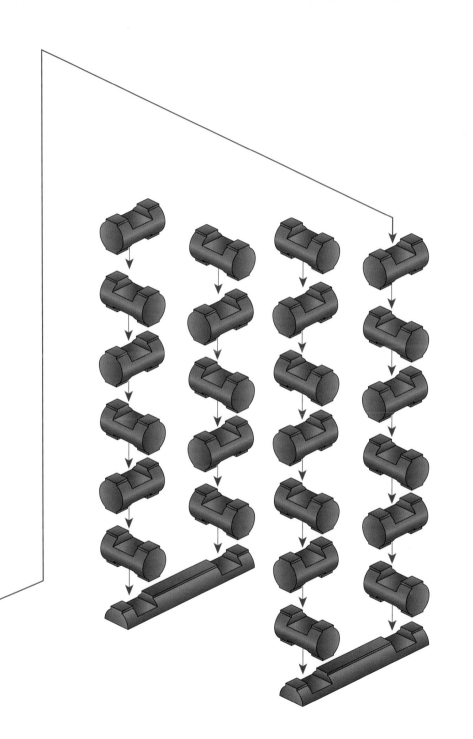

Harness Shop

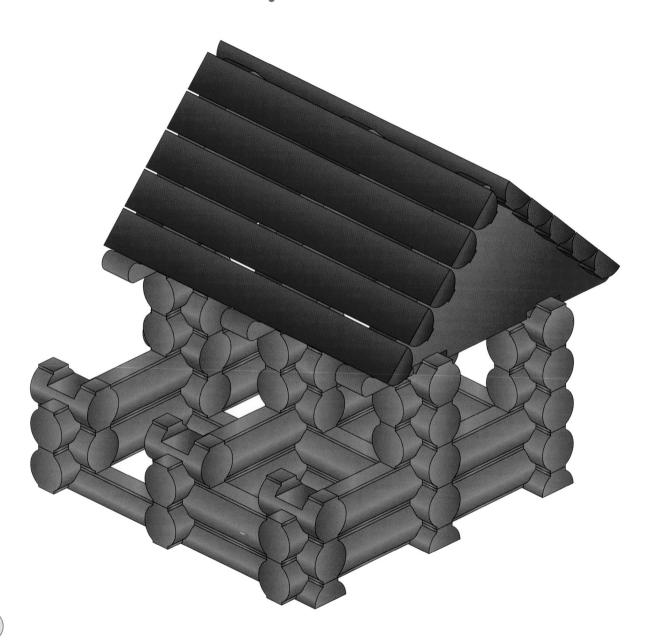

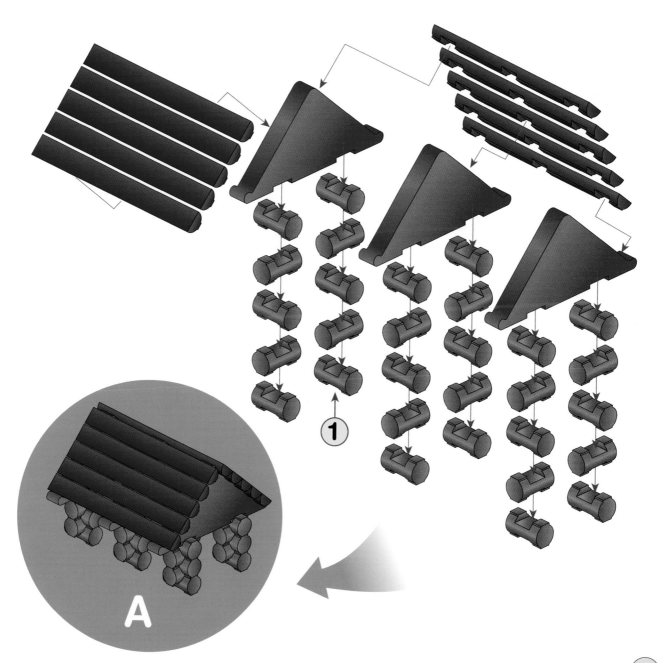

1

A

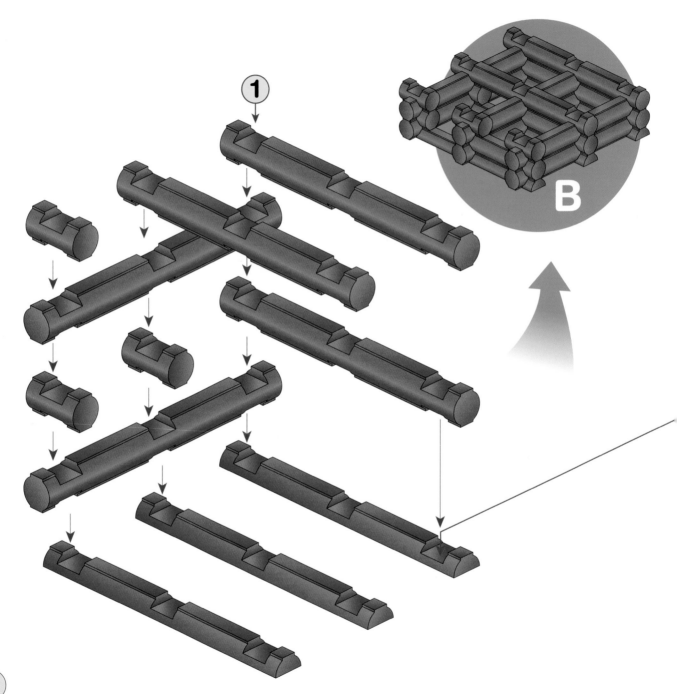

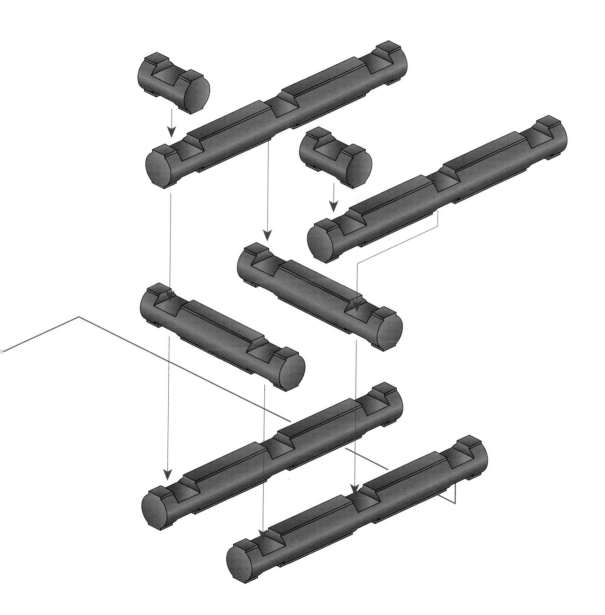

General Store

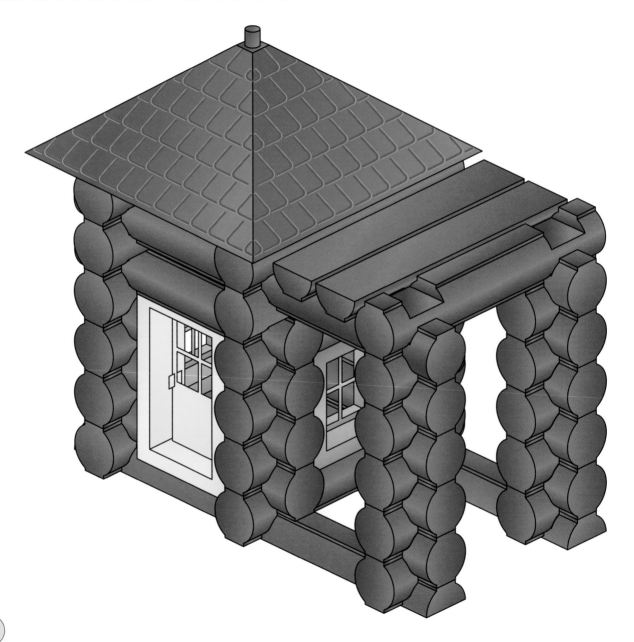

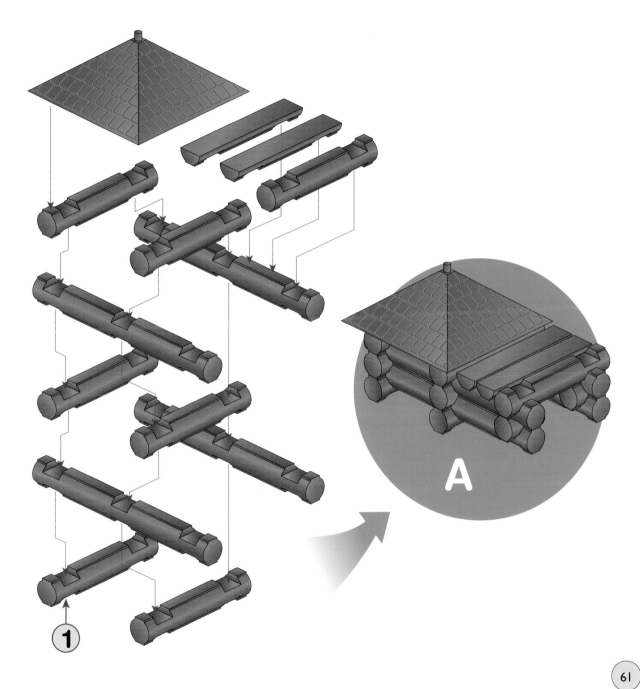

A

1

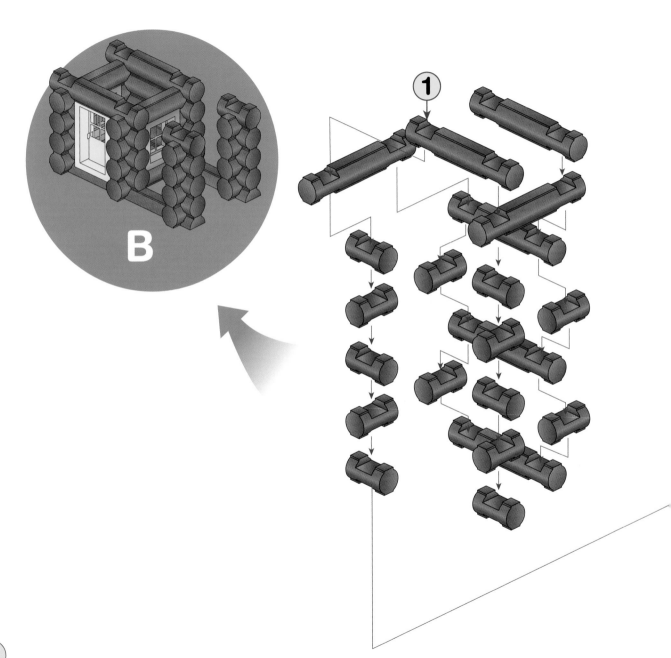

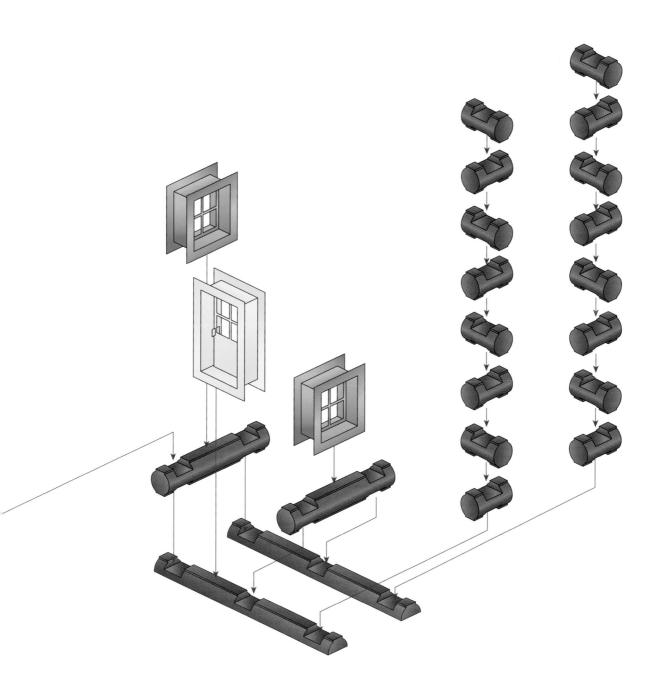

Schoolhouse

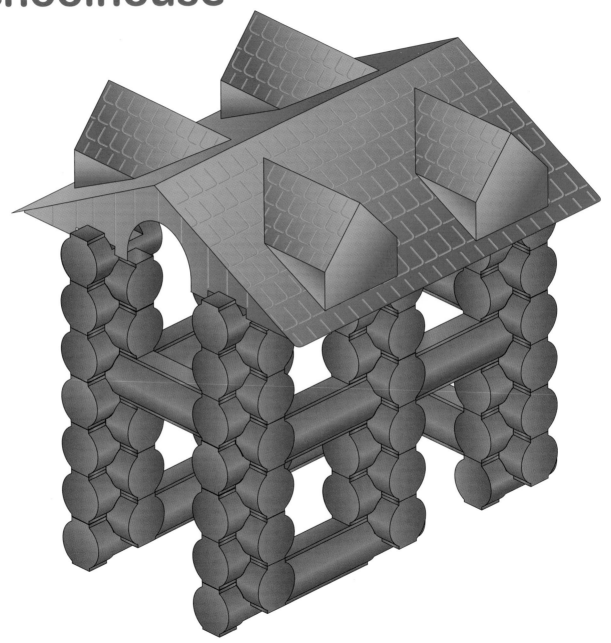

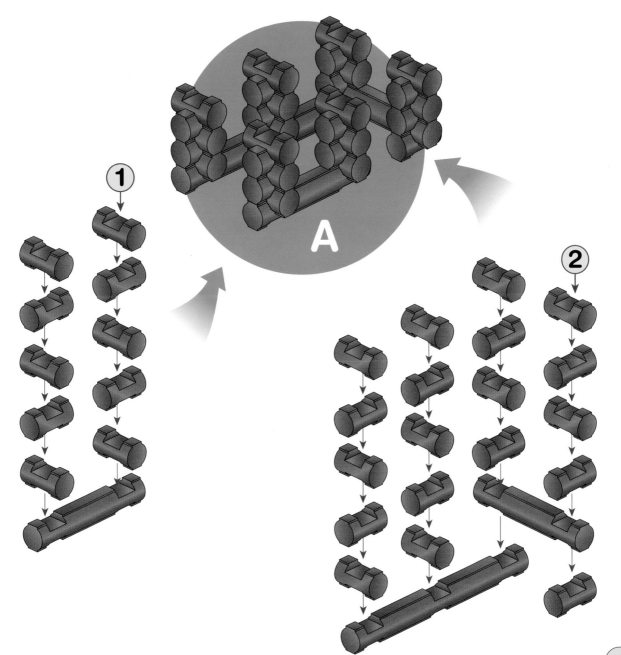

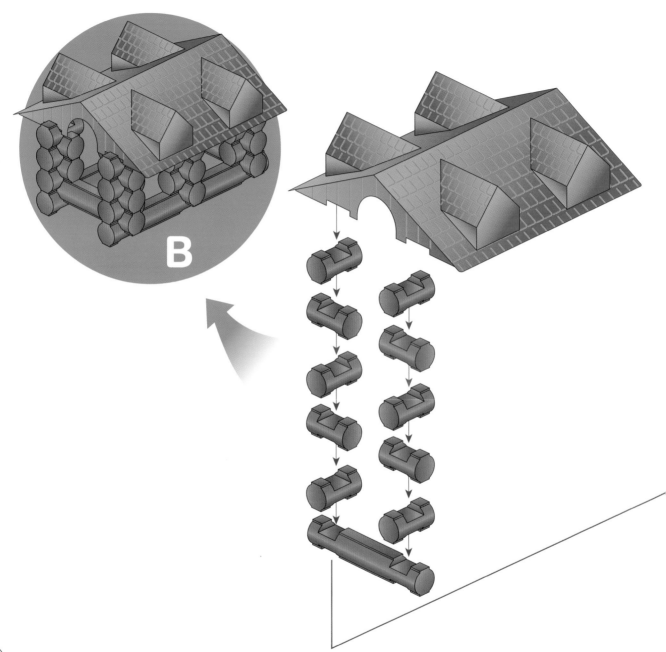

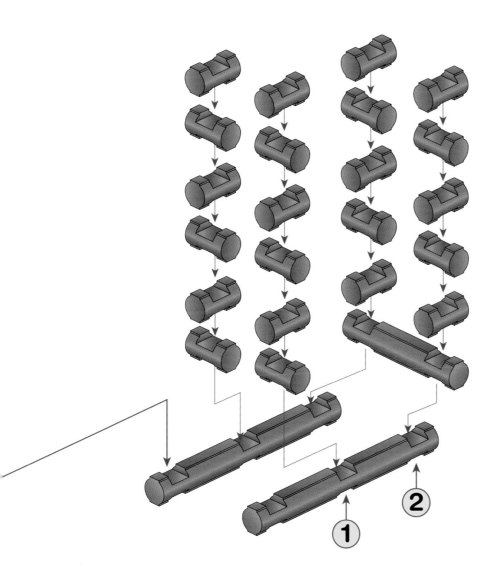

Bank

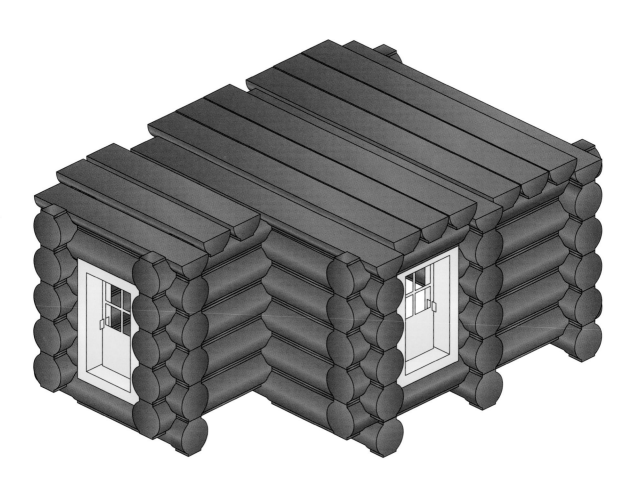

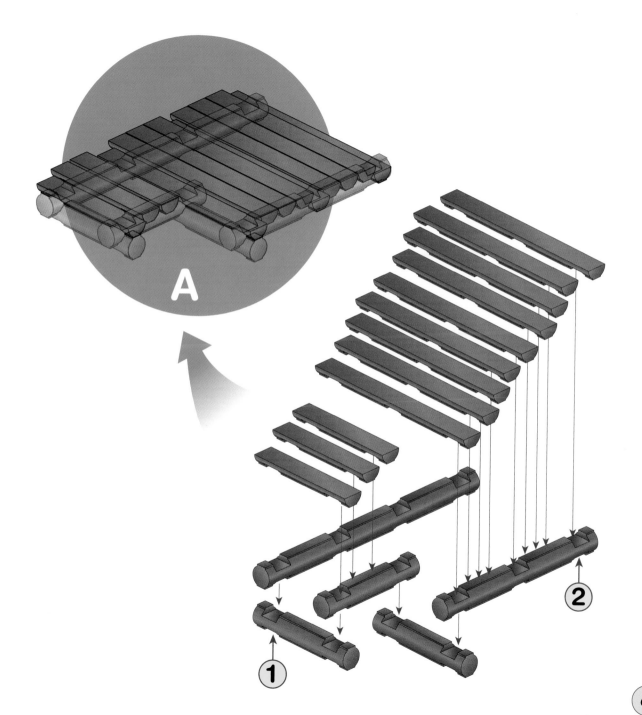

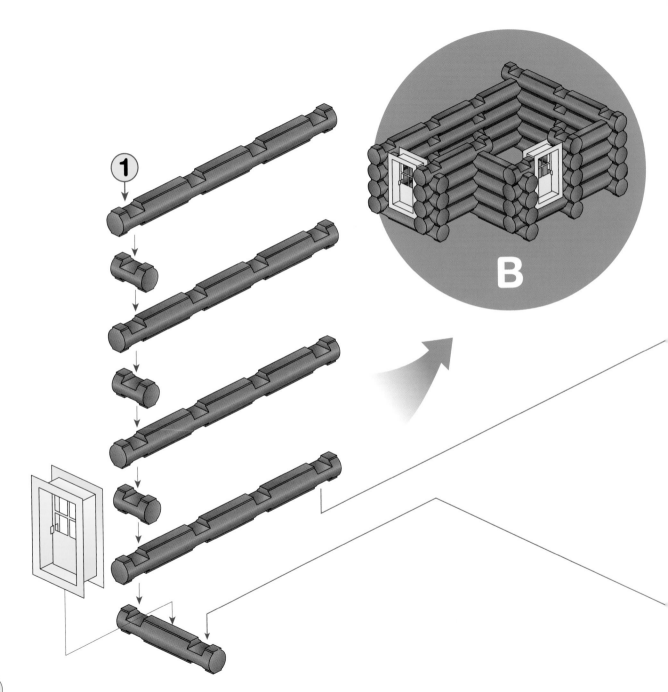

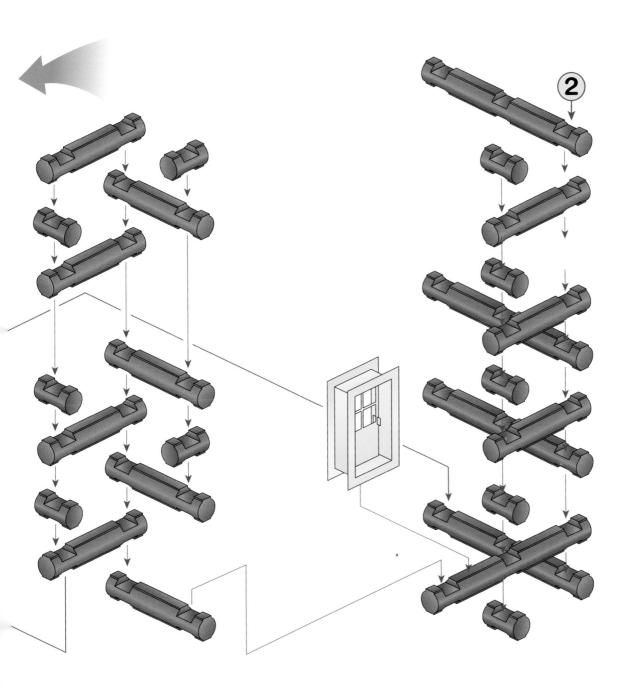

Tree House

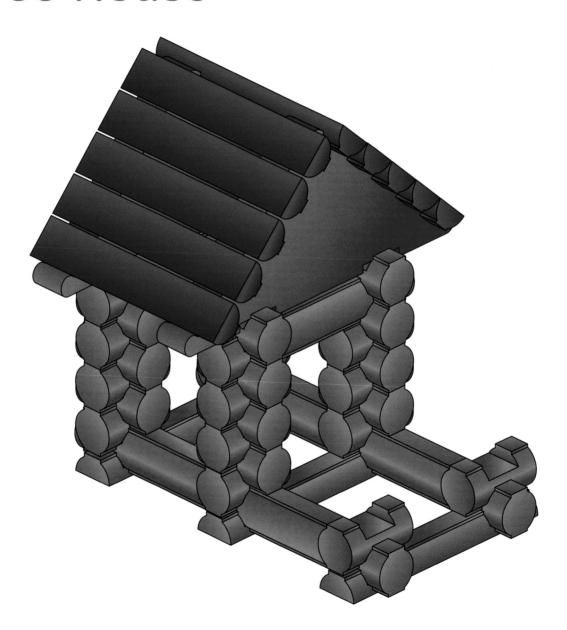

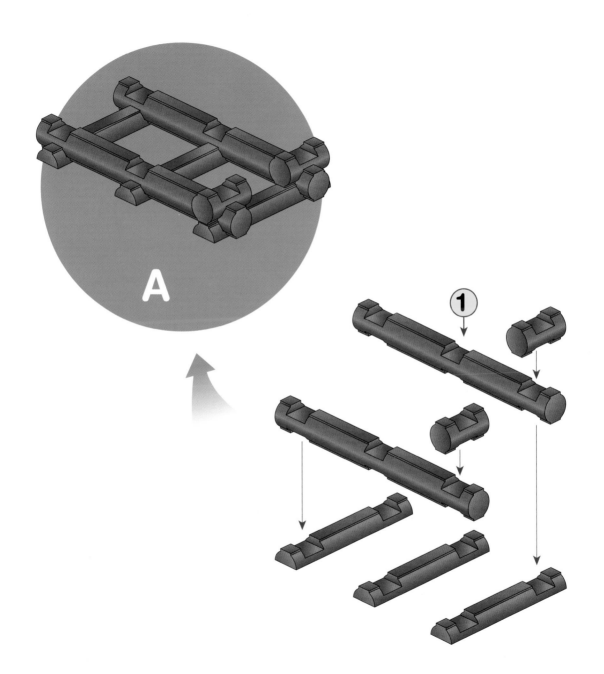

A

1

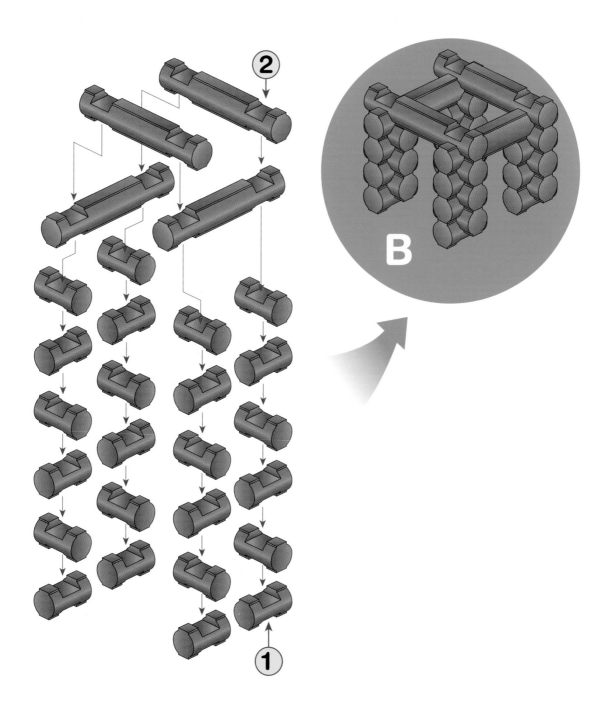

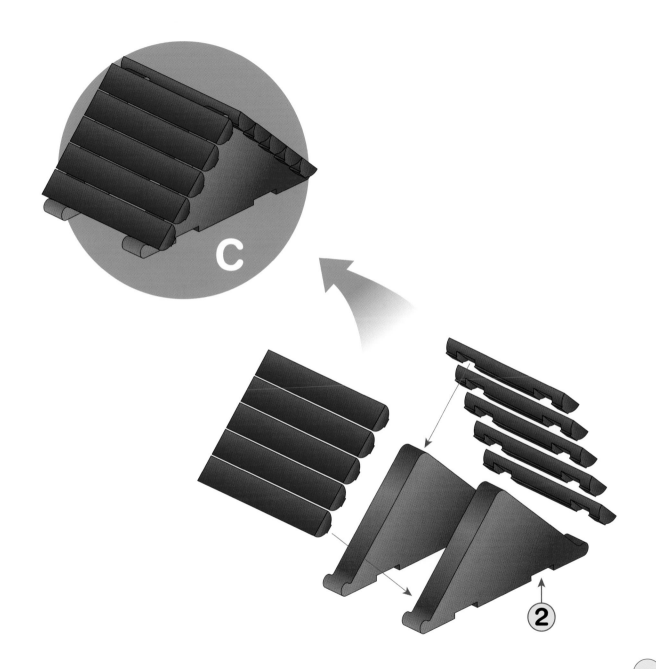

Fire Station

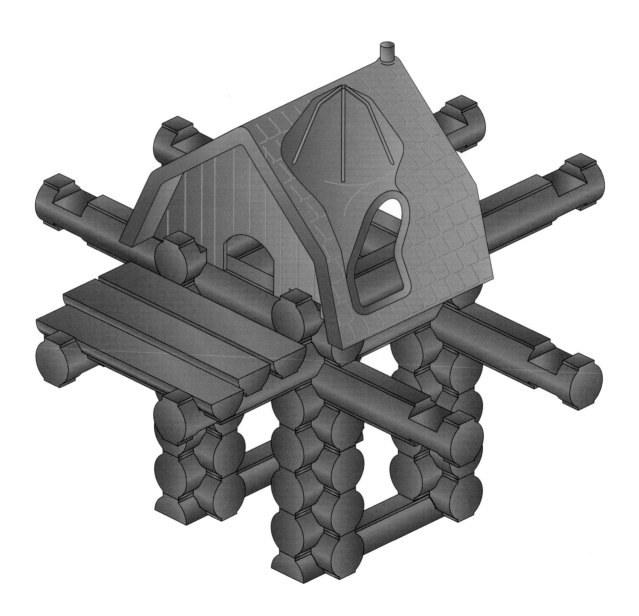

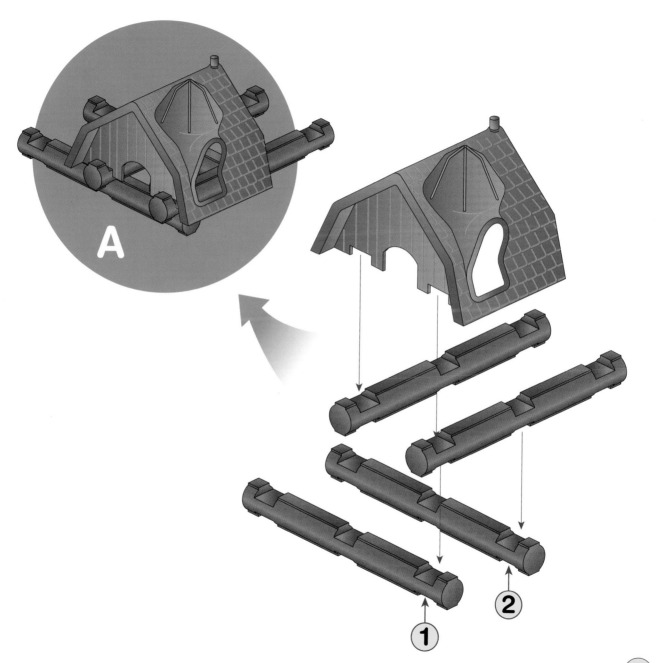

A

1

2

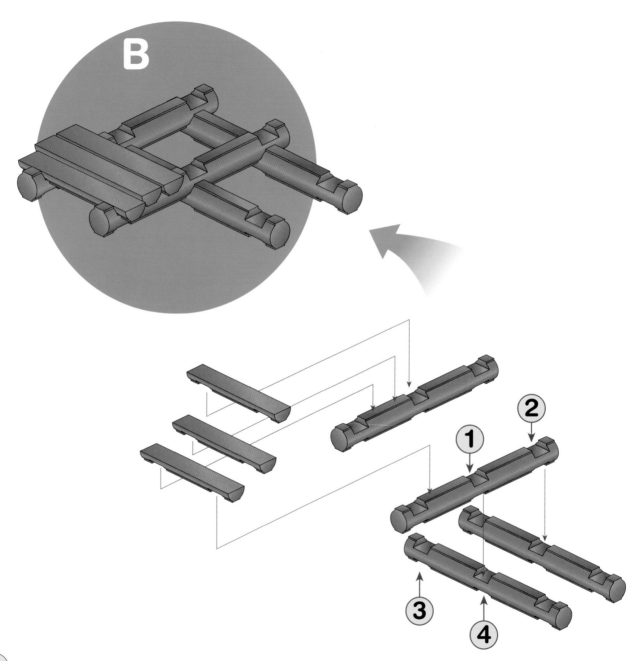

① ② ③ ④

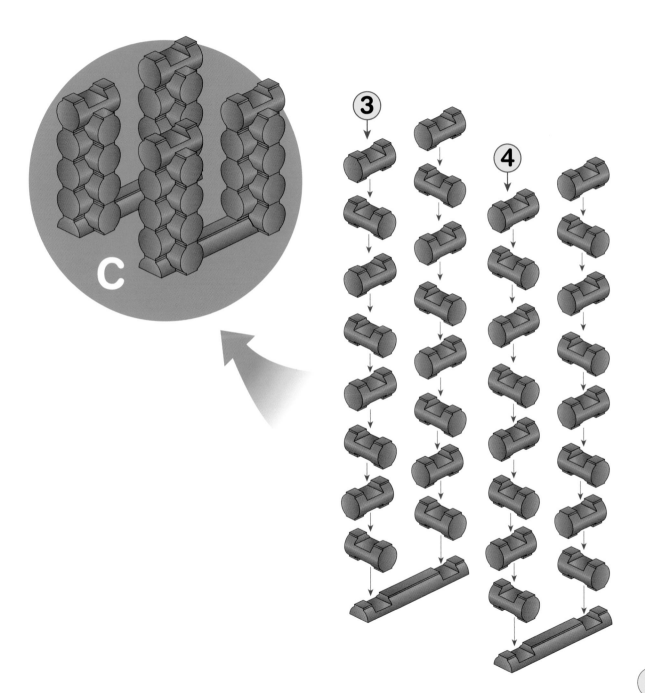

Frontier Tower

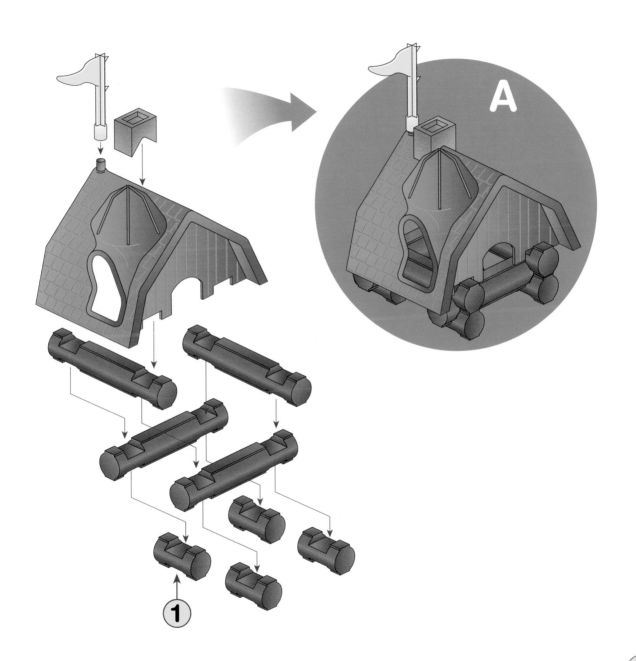

A

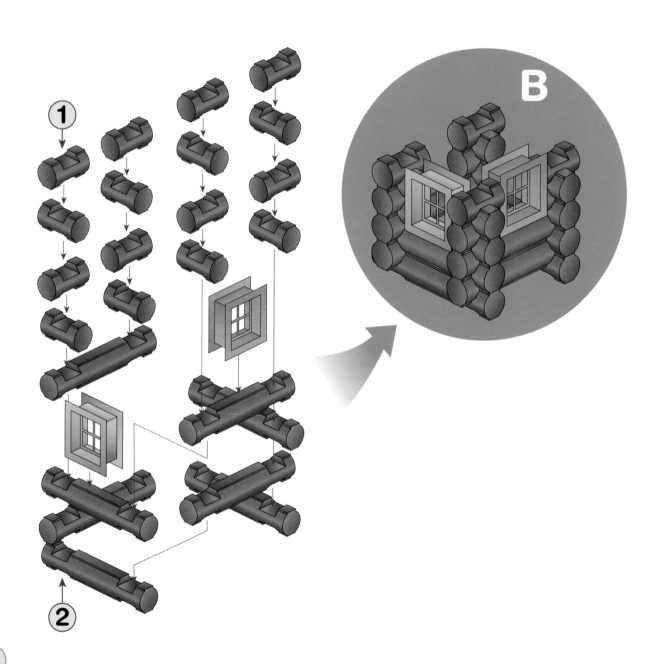

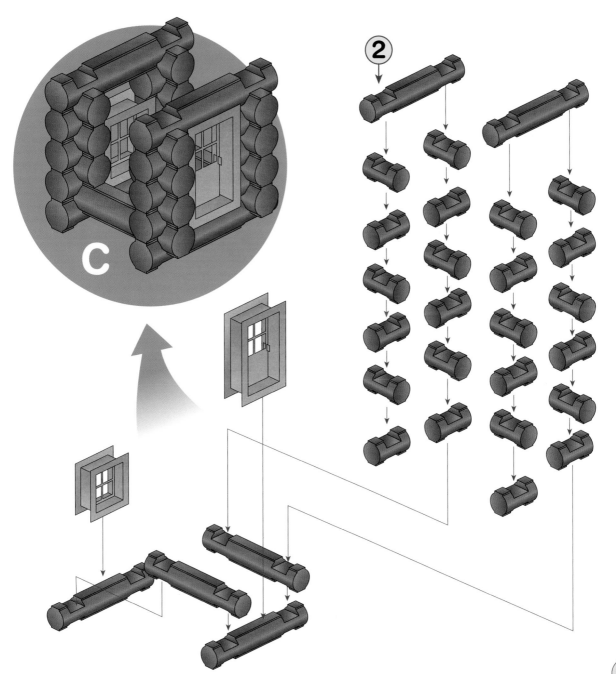

Pavilion

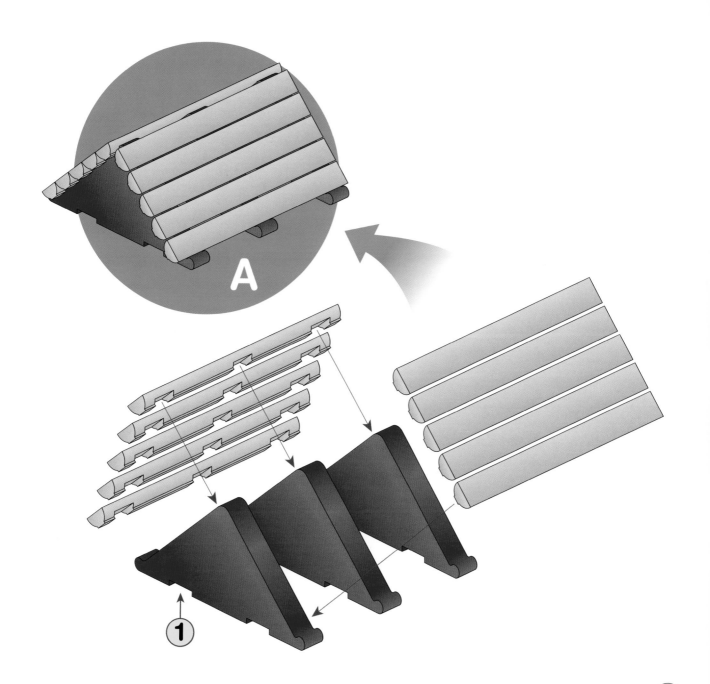

A

(1)

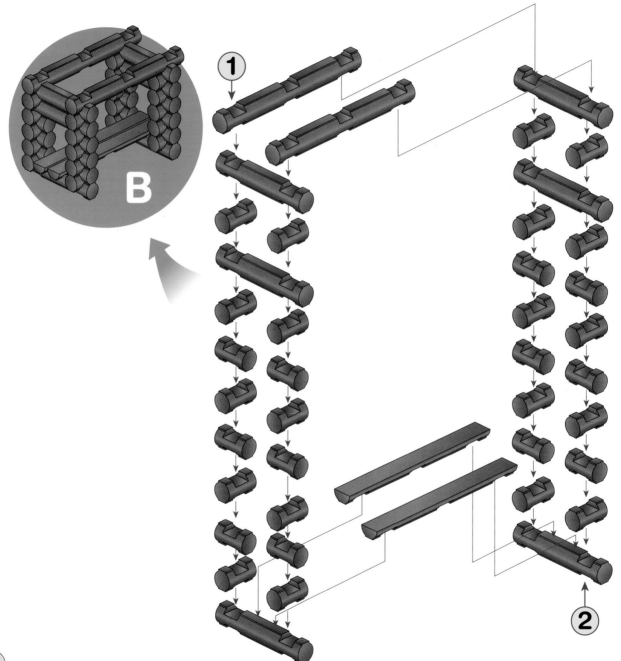

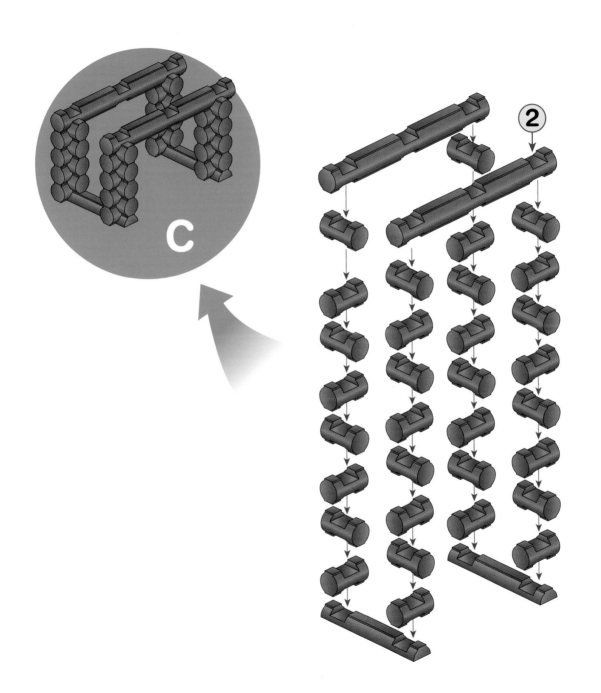

C

2

87

Sheriff's Station

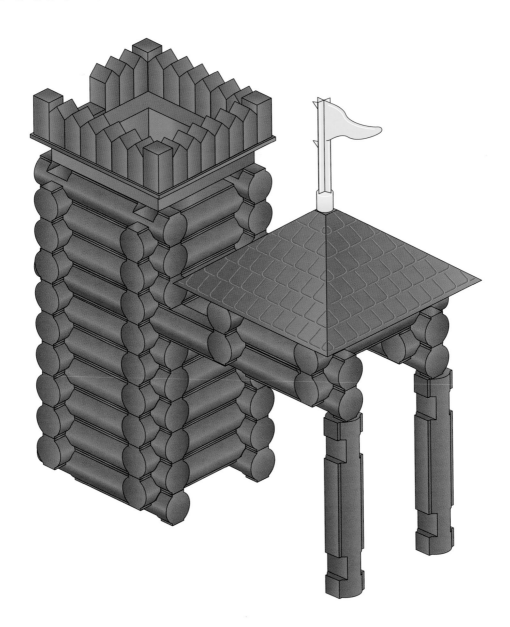

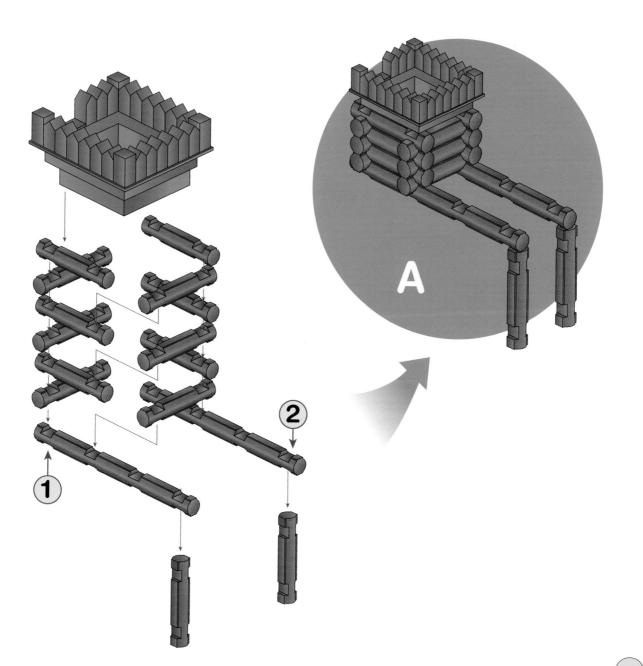

1

2

A

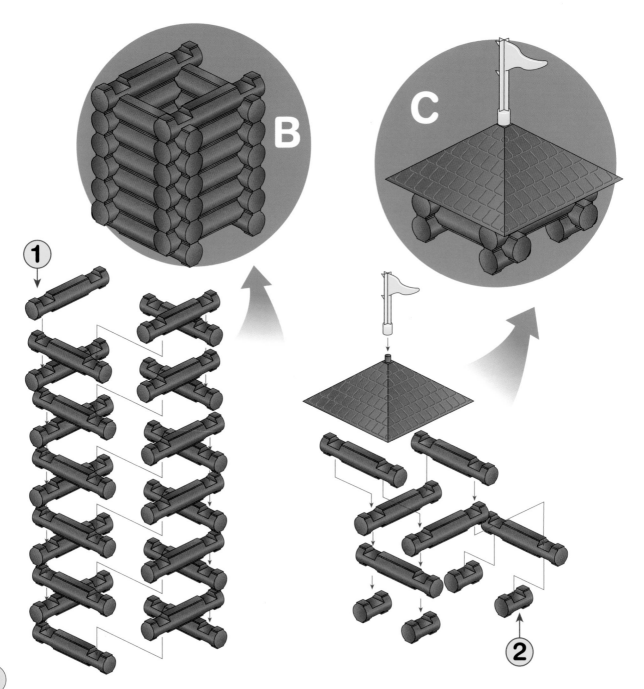

Covered Bridge

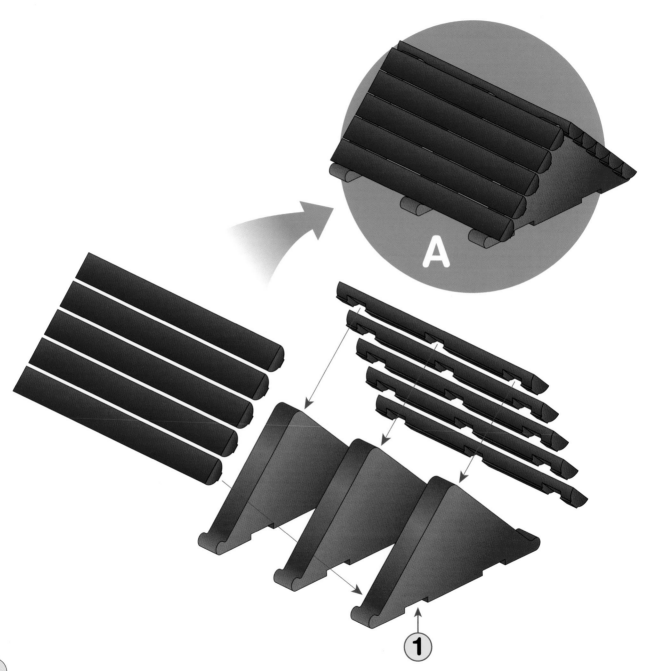

A

1

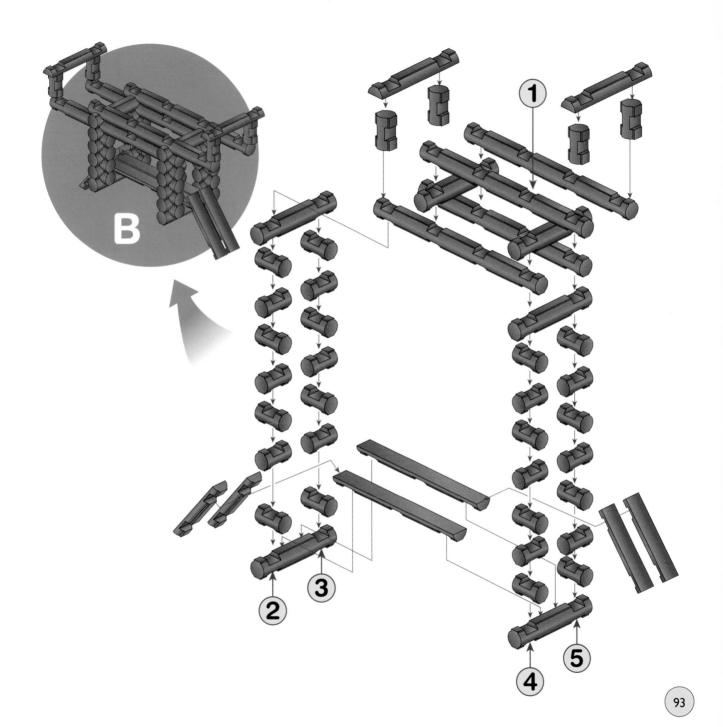

B

1

2

3

4

5

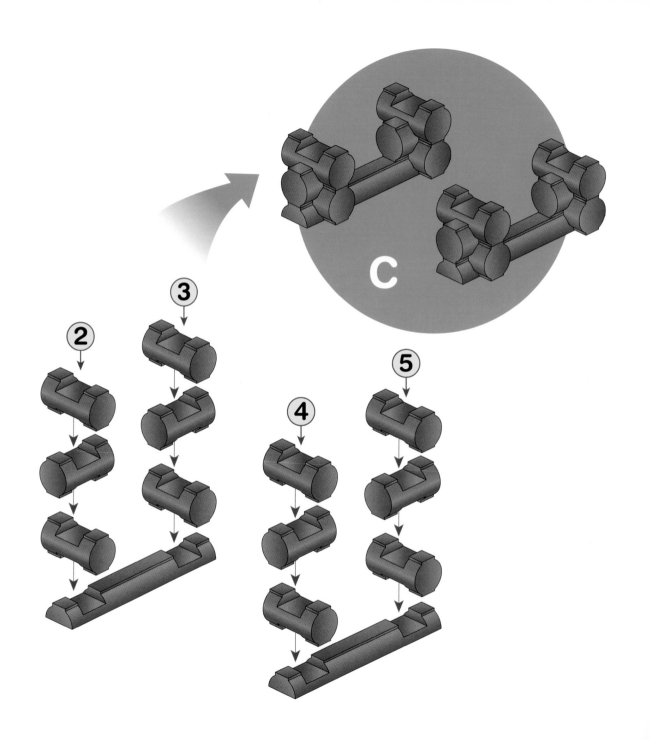

Playhouse

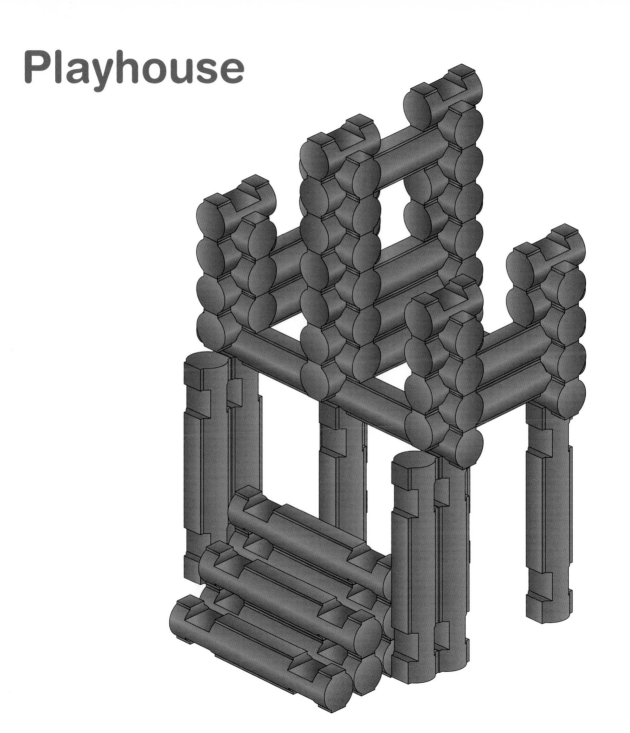

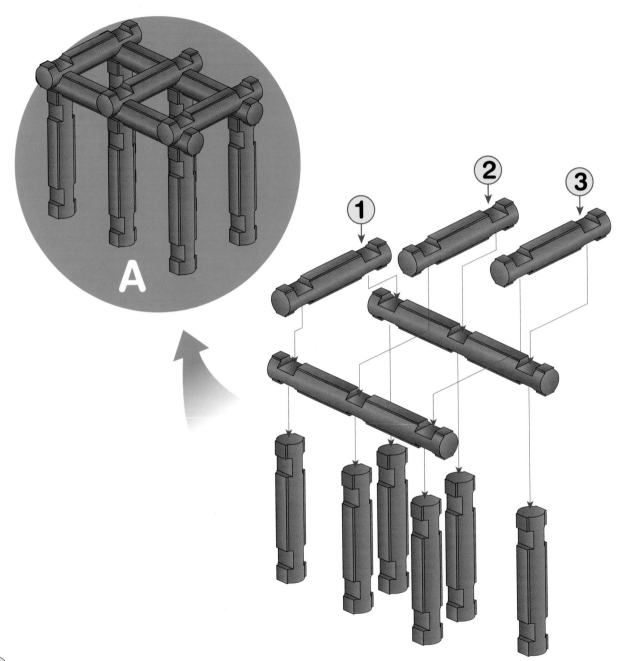

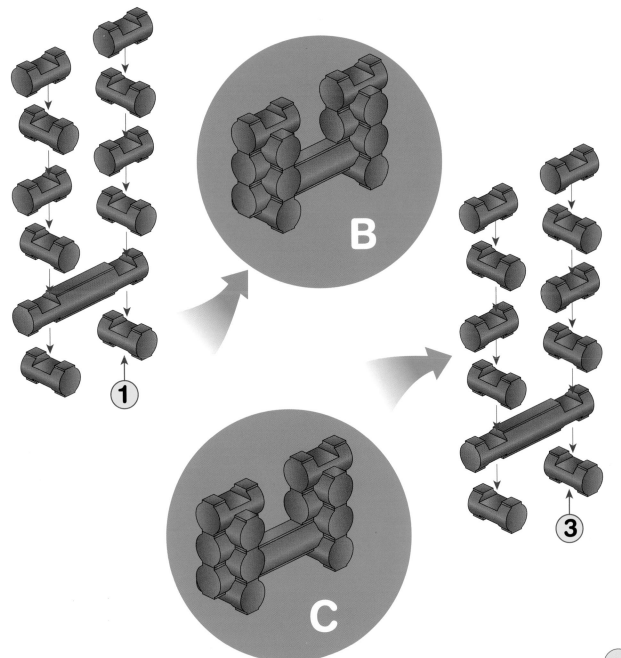

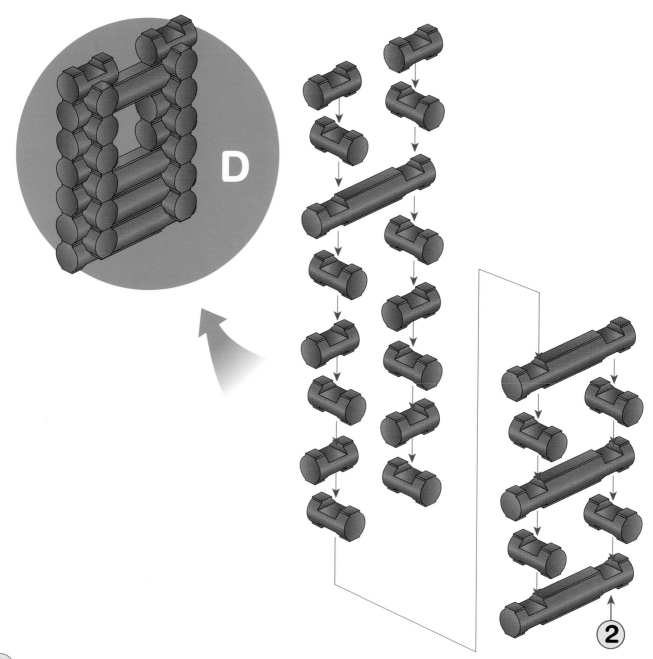

D

2

Lighthouse

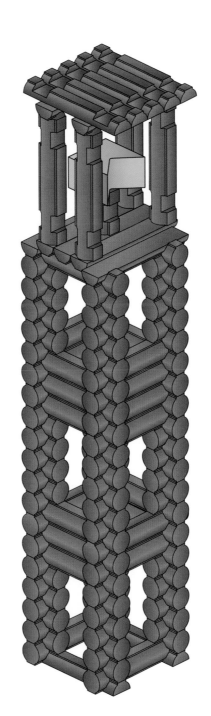

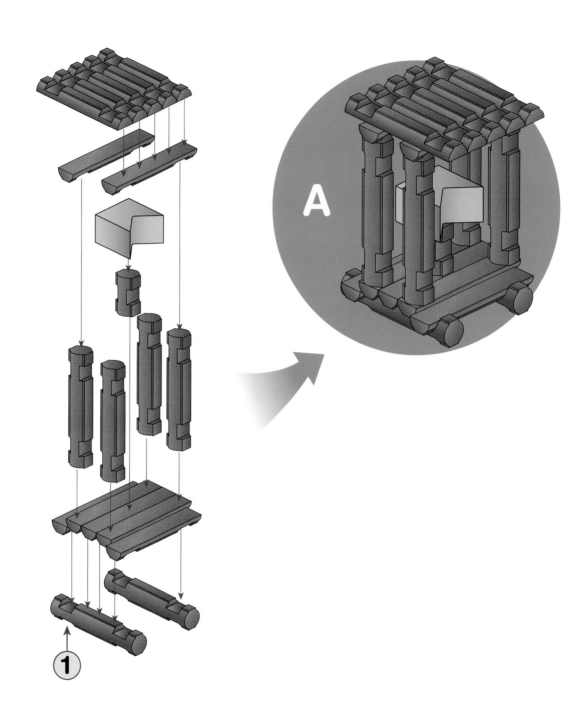

A

1

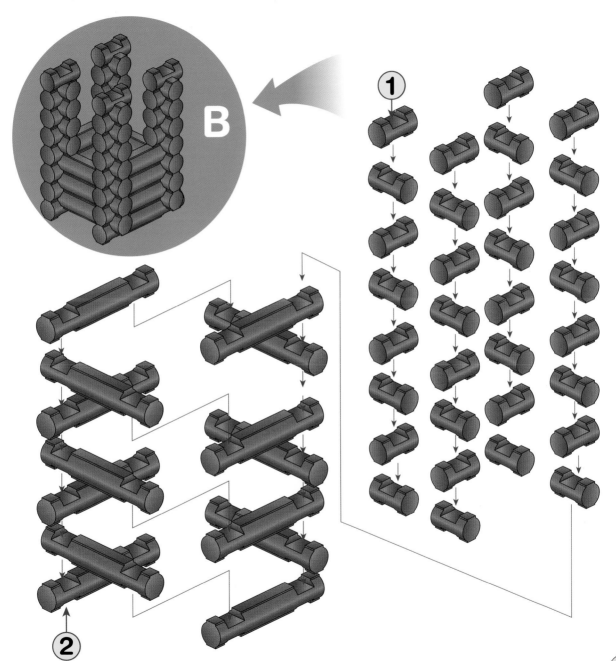

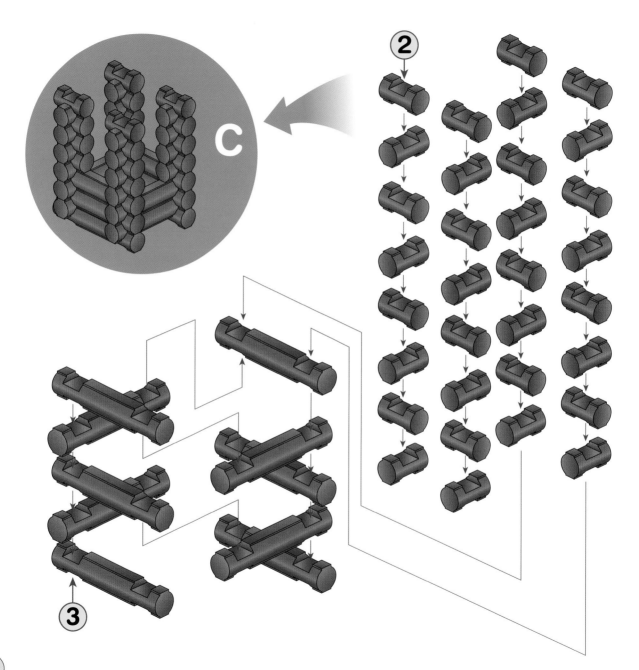

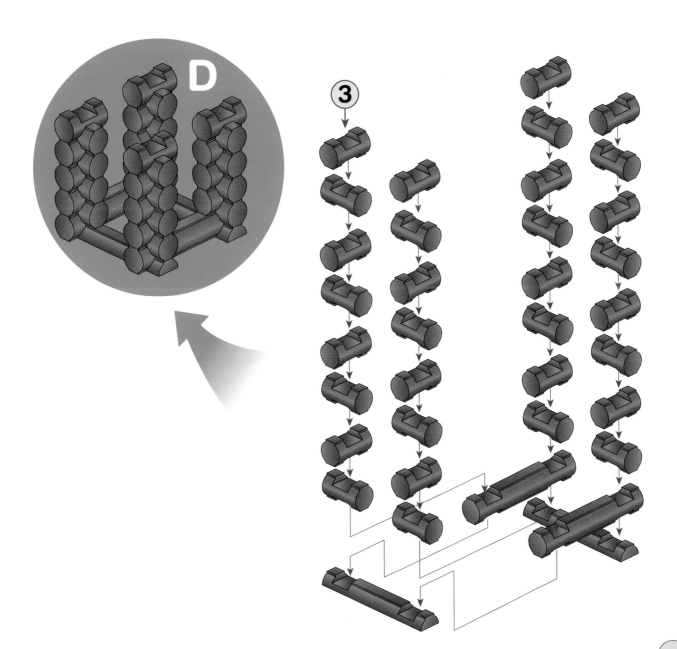

Toll Booth

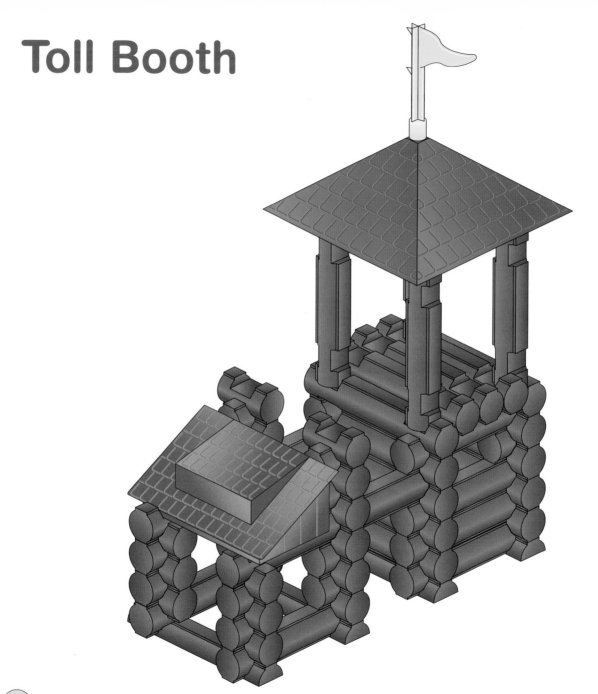

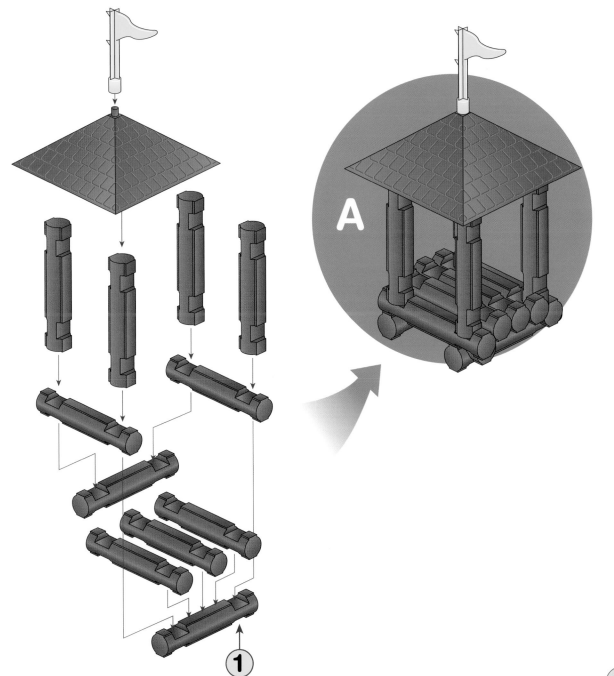

A

1

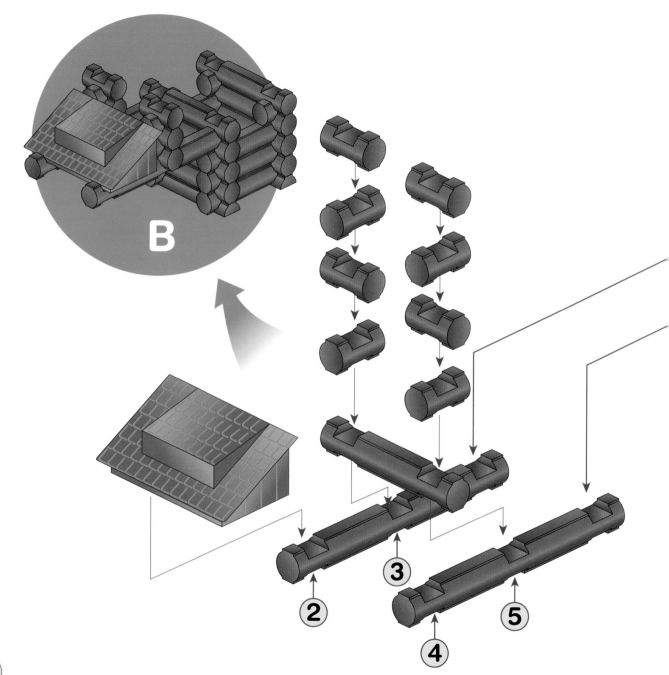

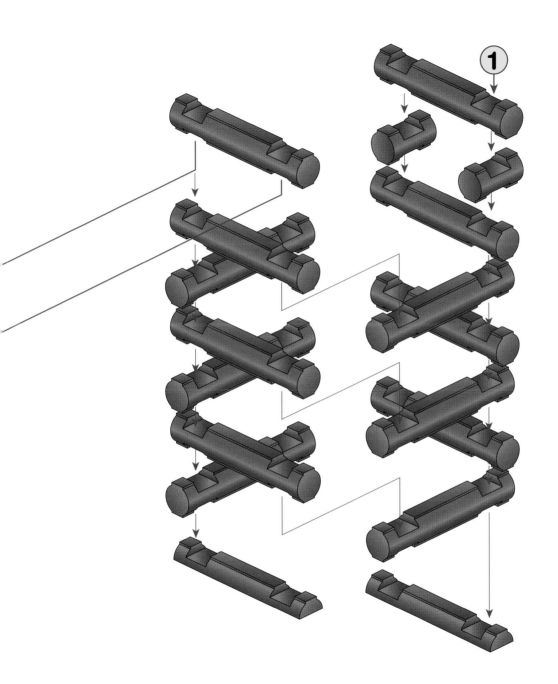

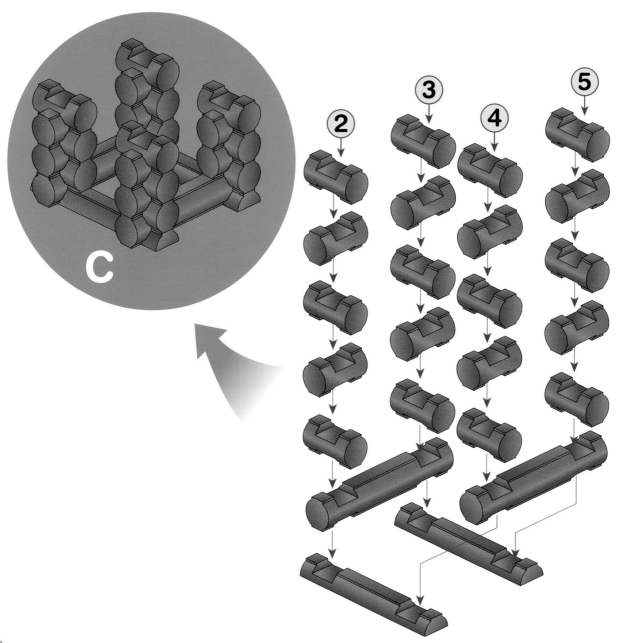

Watchtower

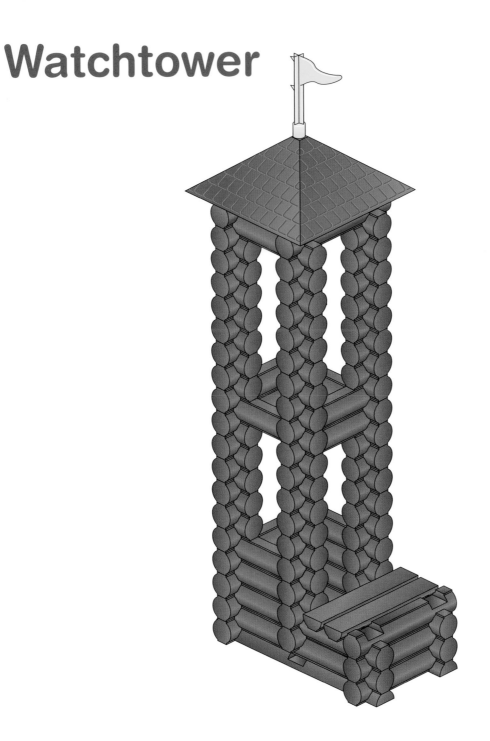

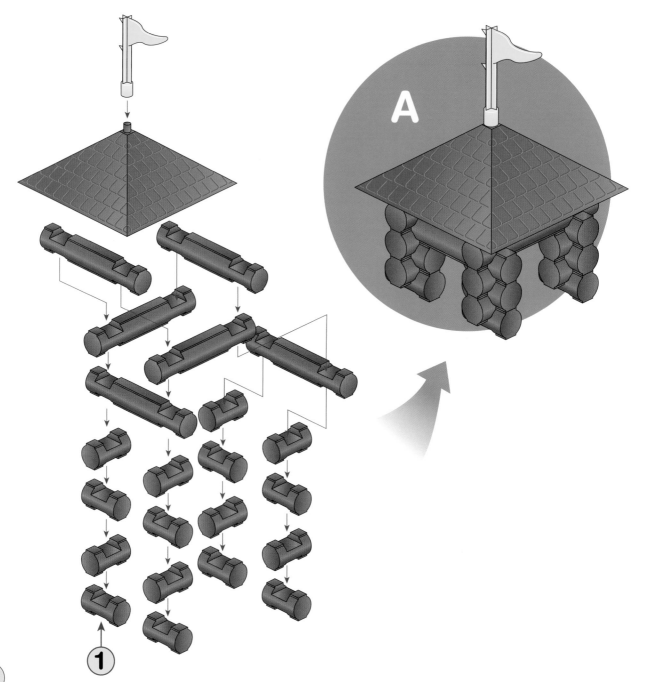

1

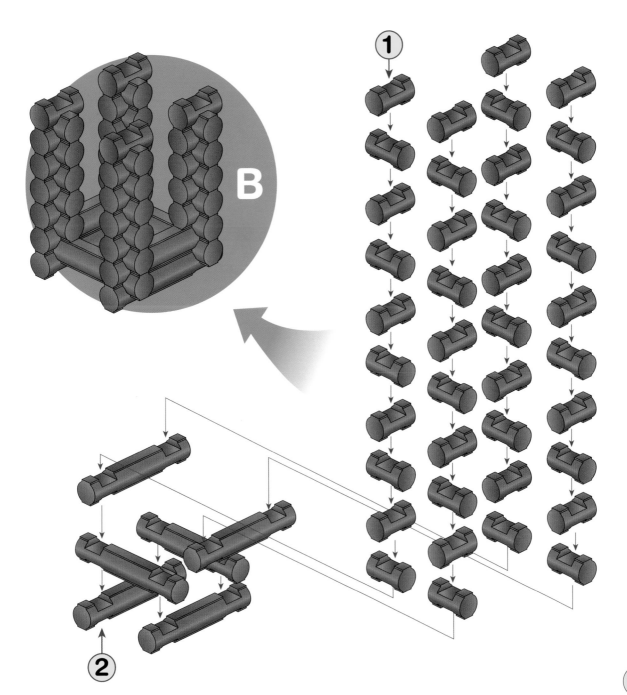

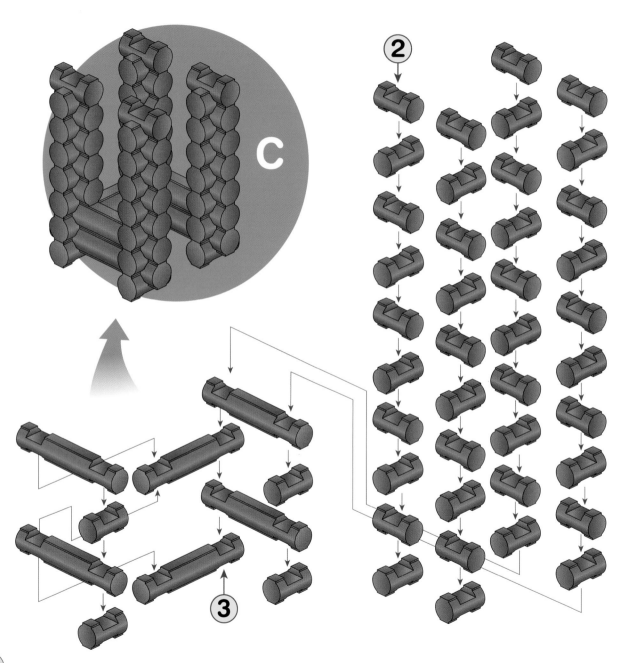

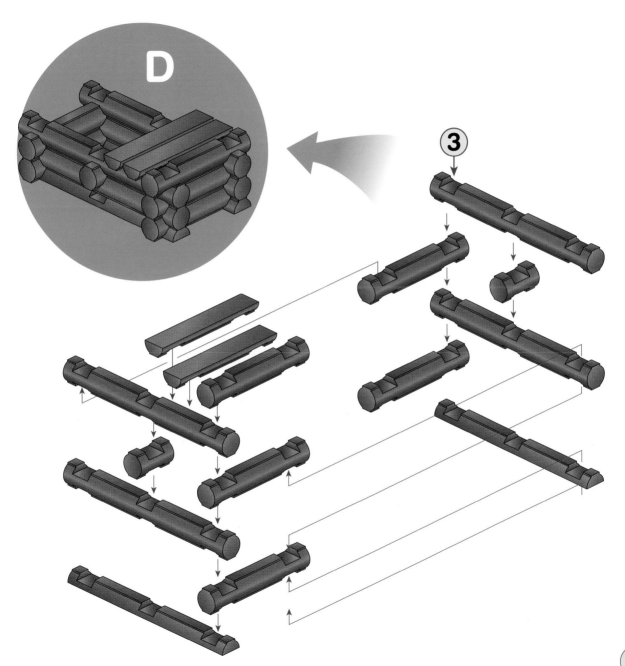

D

③

Farmhouse

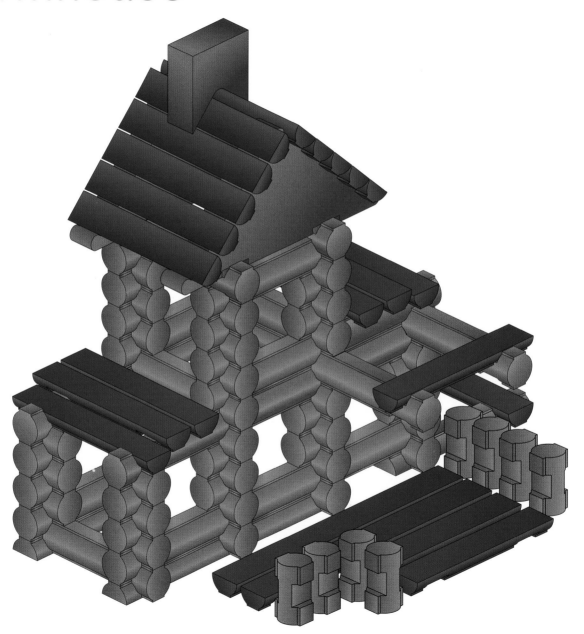

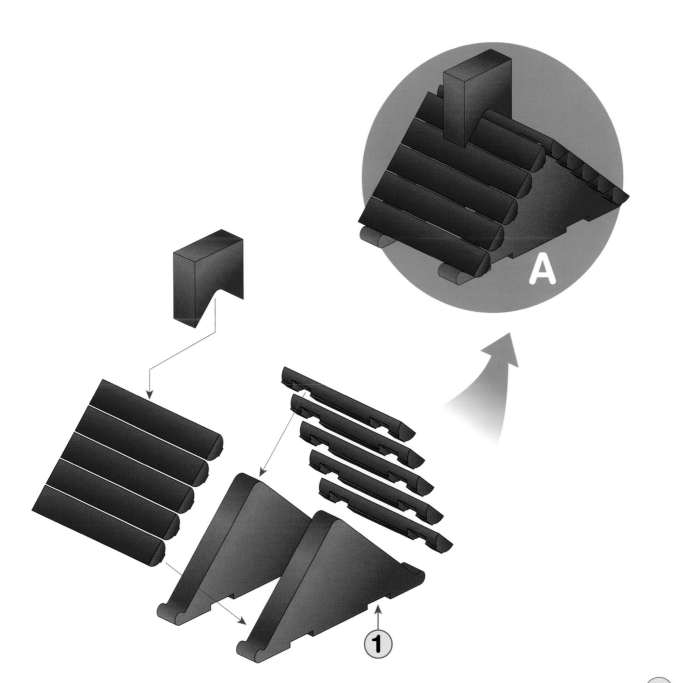

A

1

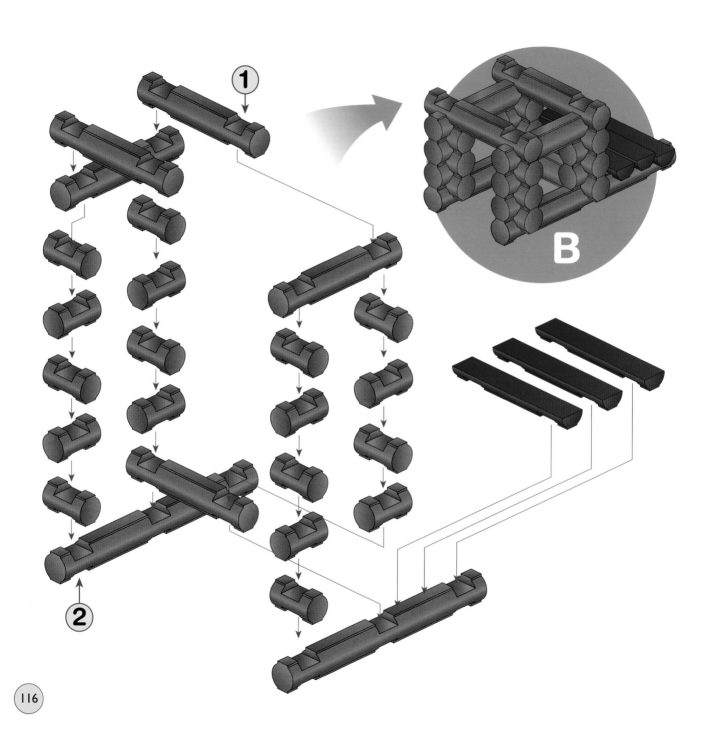

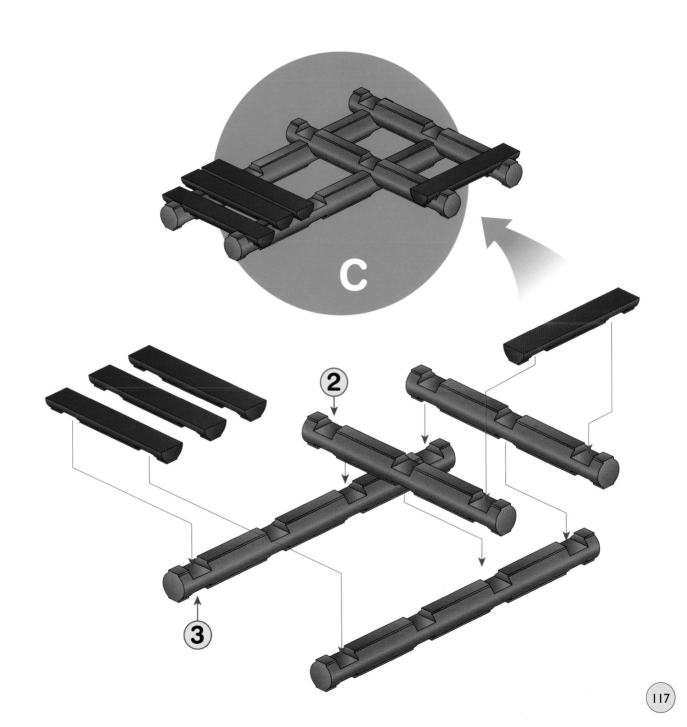

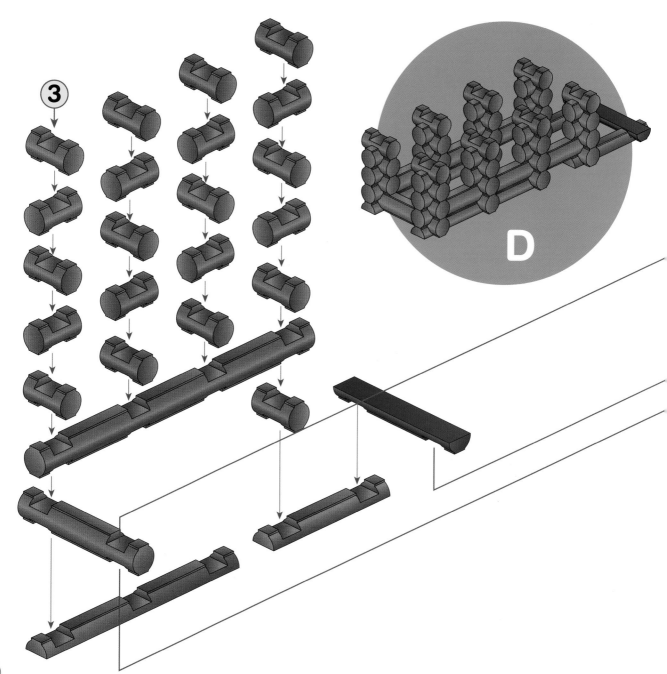

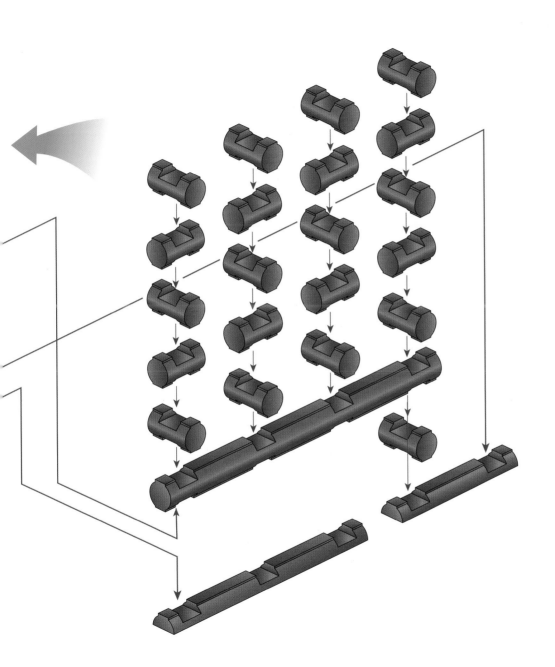

Barn

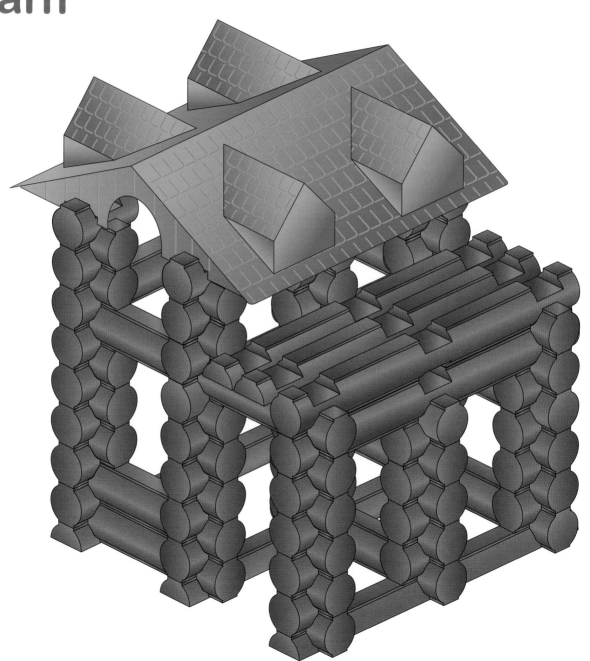

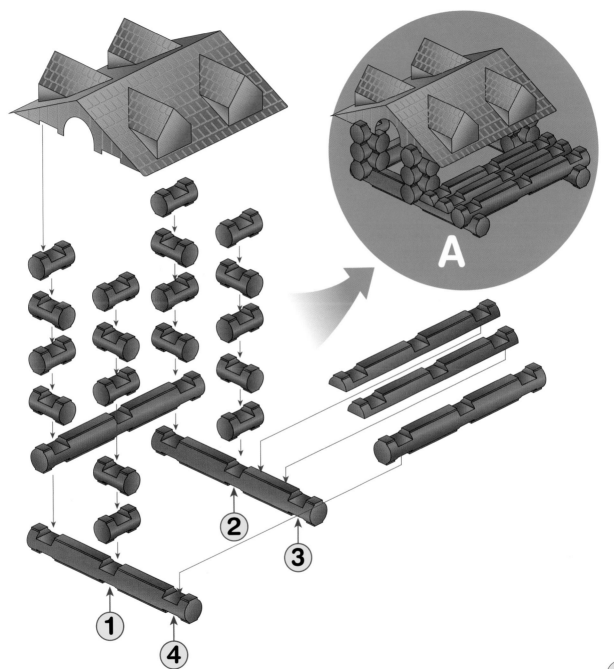

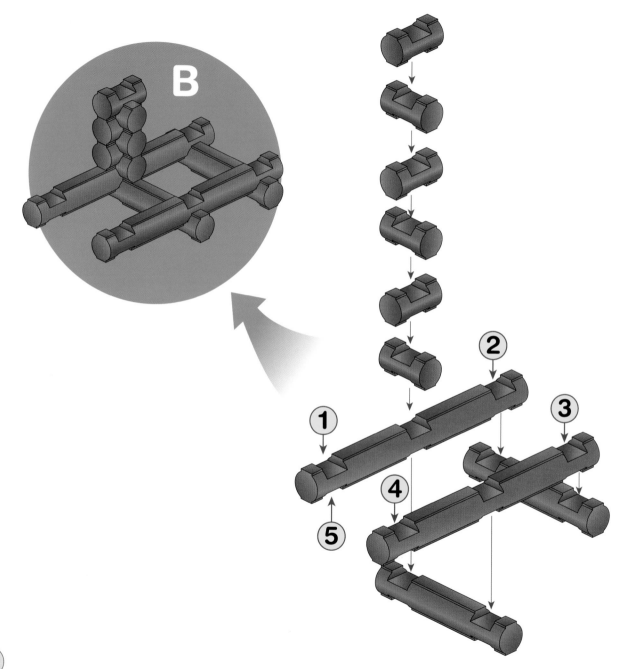

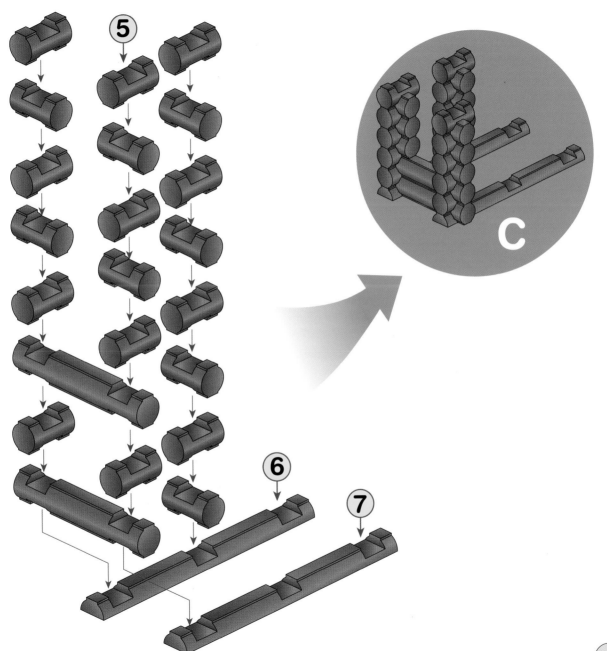

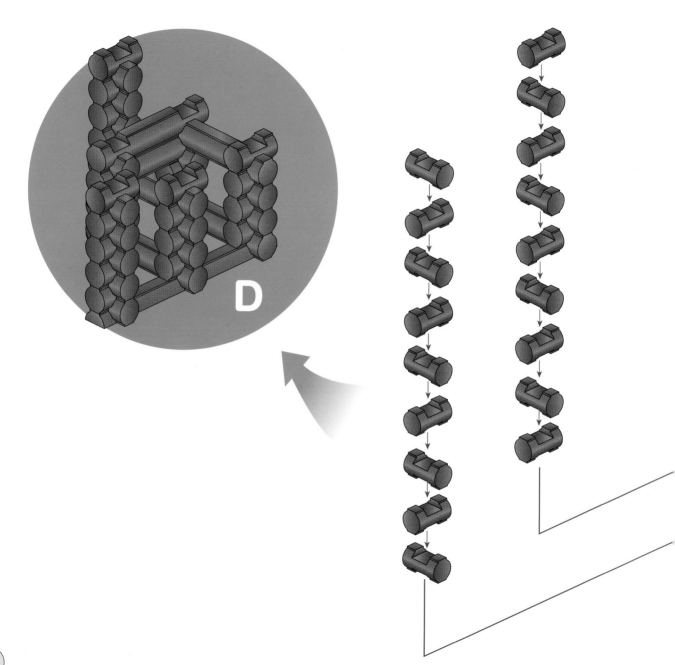

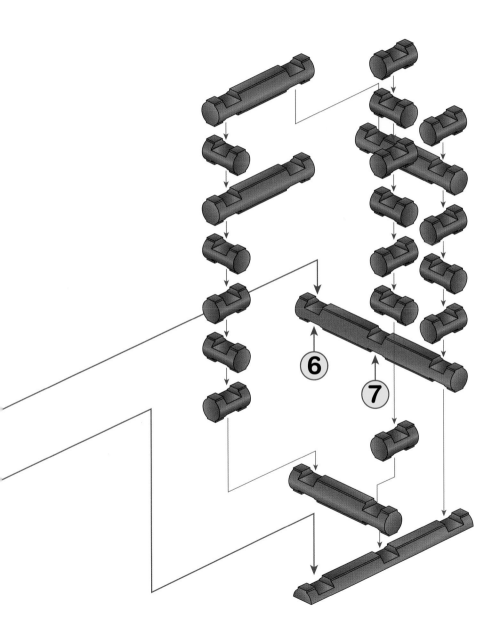

Ponderosa

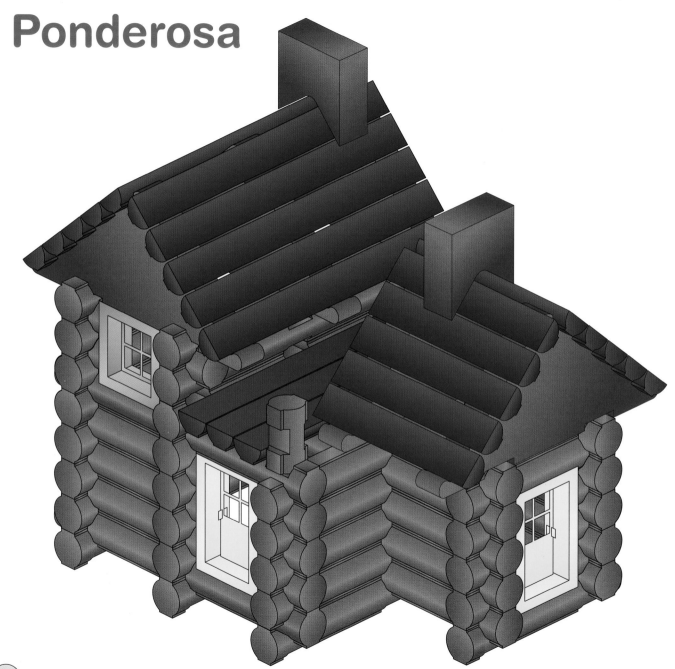

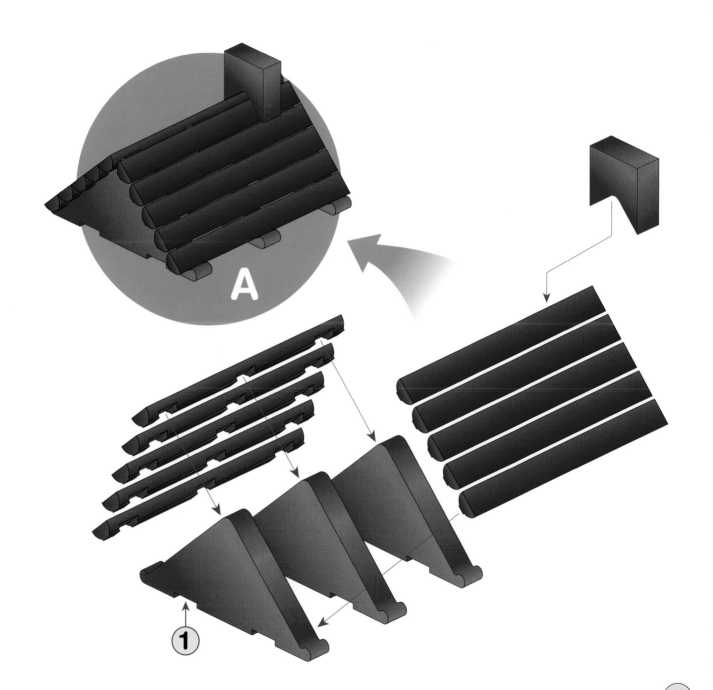

A

1

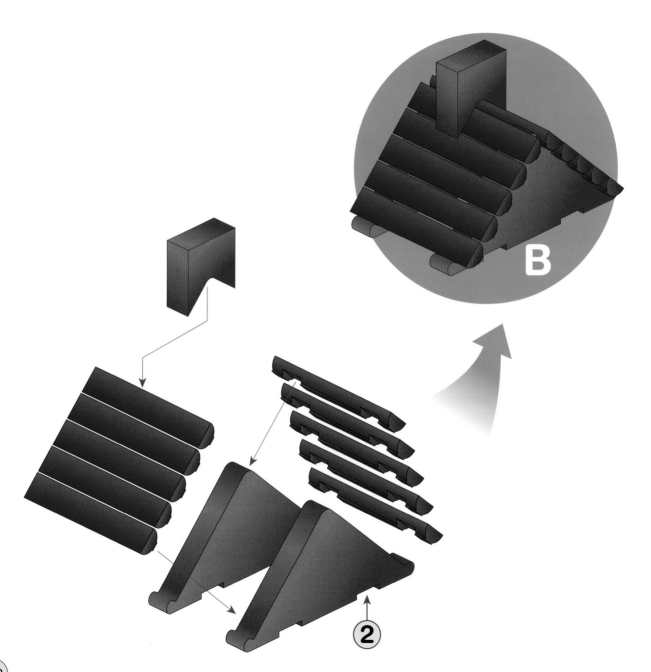

B

2

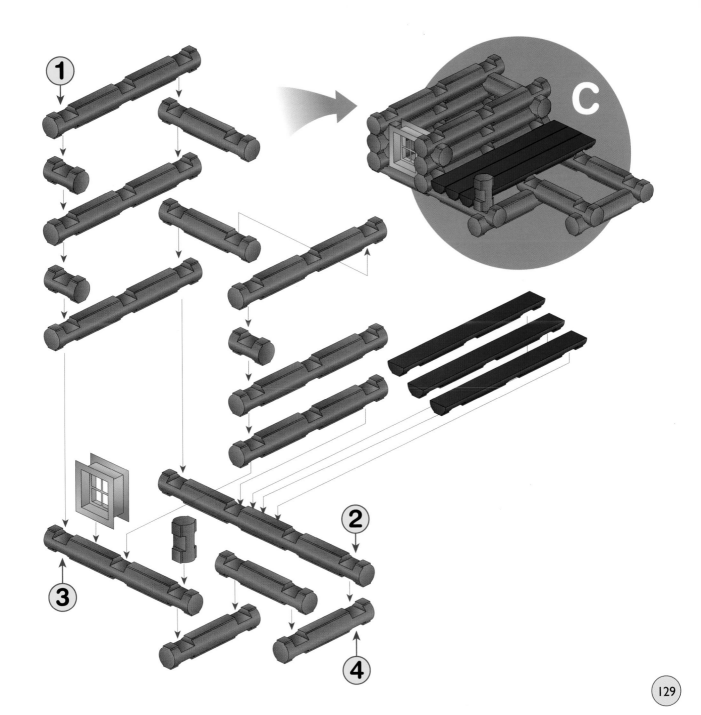

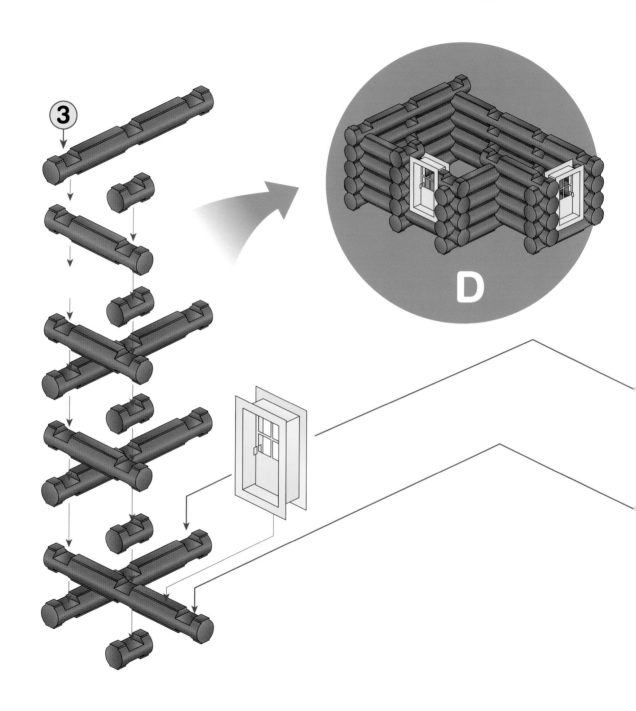

D

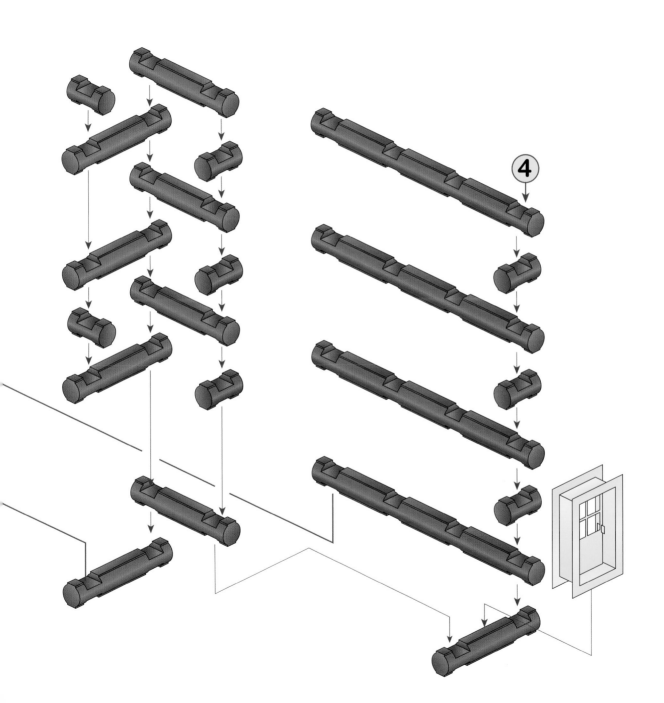

4

Pagoda

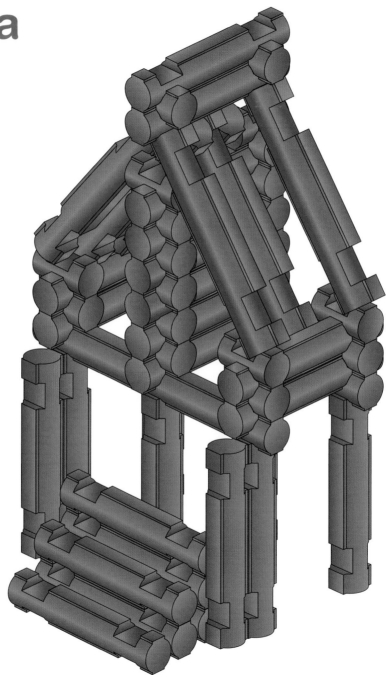

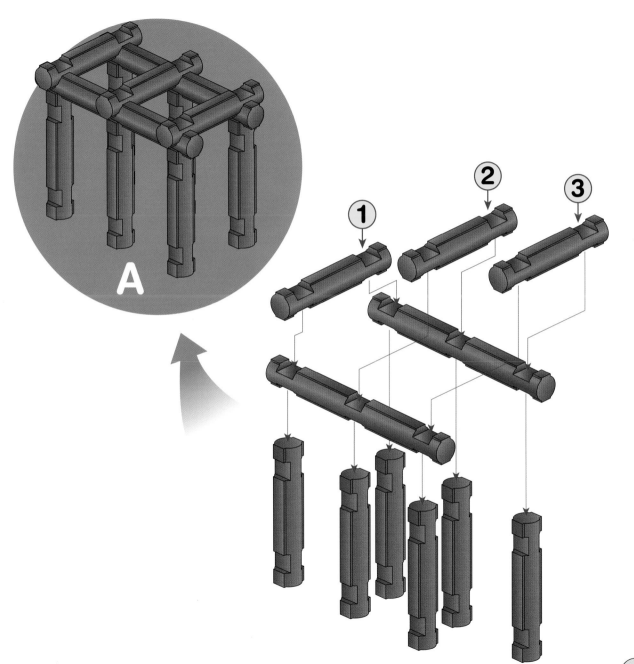

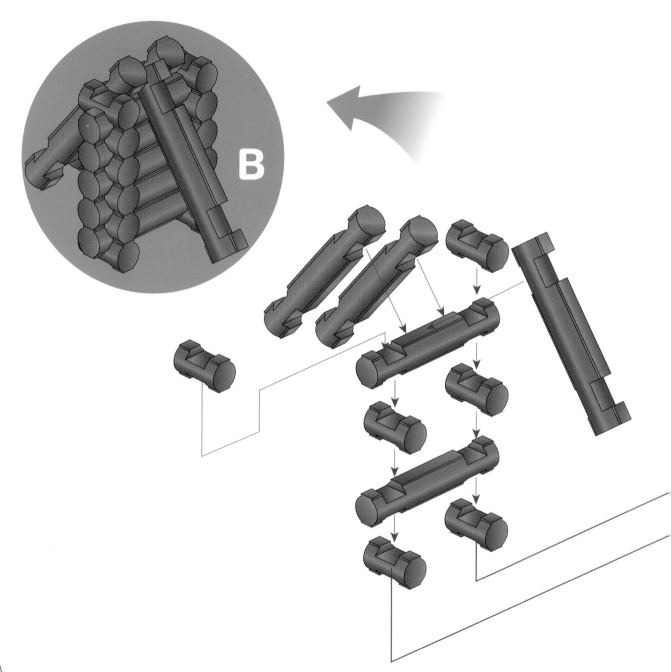

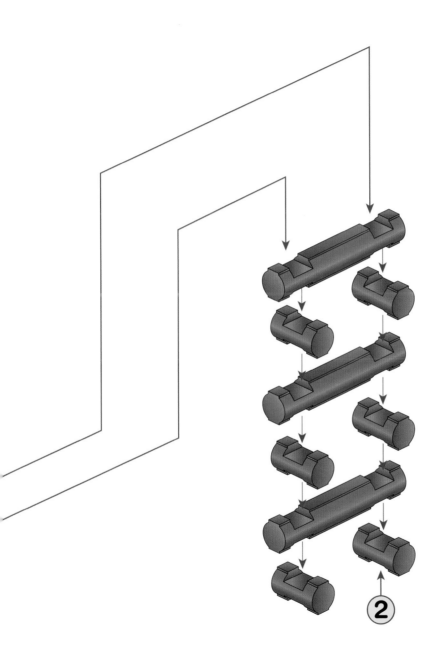

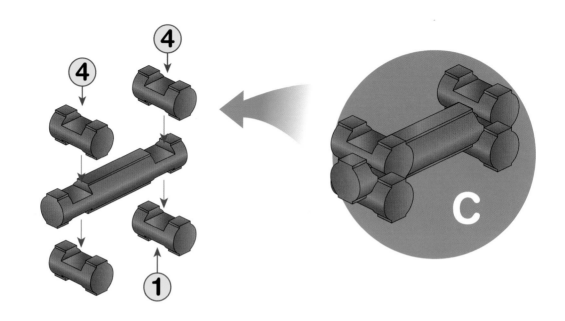

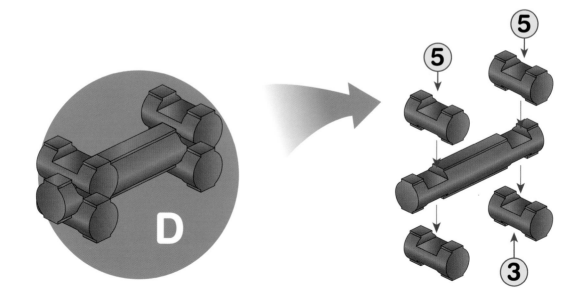

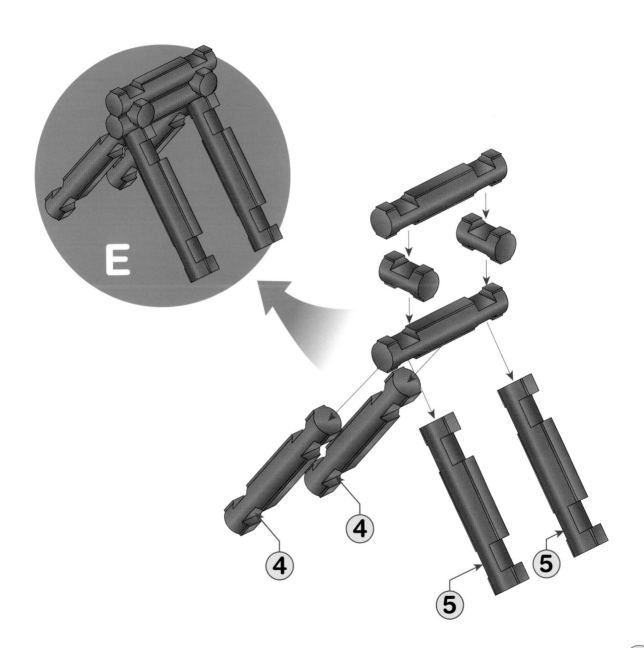

E

4

4

5

5

5

Bell Tower

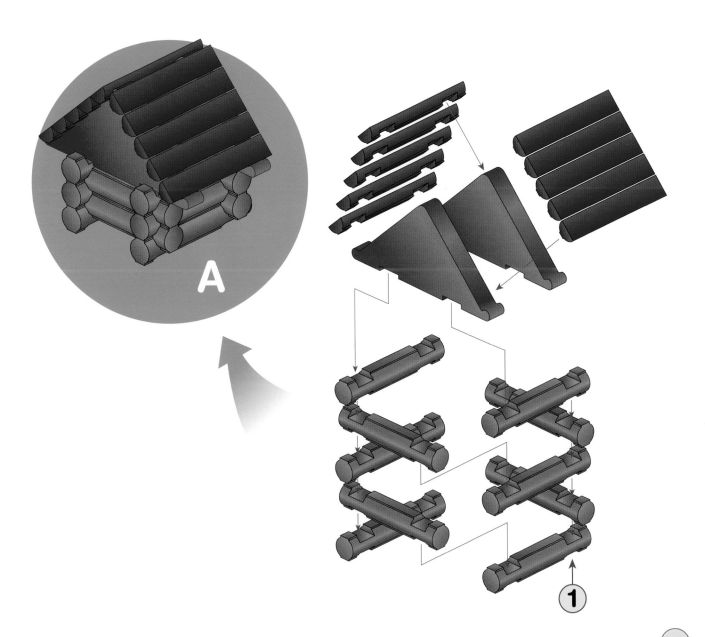

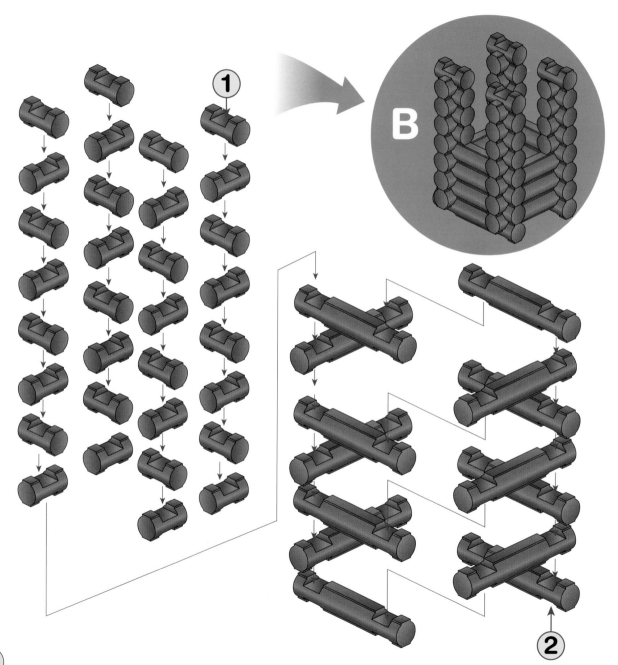

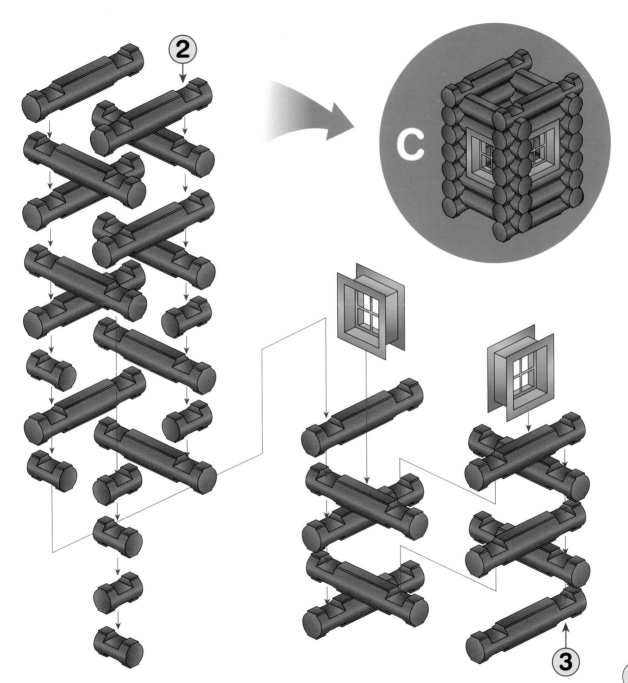

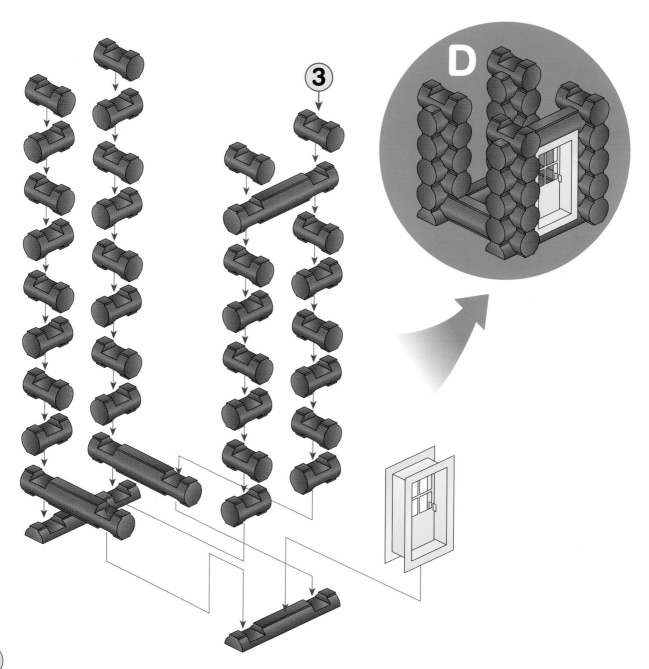